Praise for

Second Chance at Love: A Practical Guide to Remarriage after Loss

Shirley Mozena is uniquely qualified to address the challenges and loneliness of grief and loss. I have seen her, alongside her husband, Jim, provide nurturing and life-giving counsel and hope through the GriefShare ministry. I have read several of her books and materials, which have already impacted many lives. Her heart for those who are hurting is only matched by her personal experience with grief and loss and remarriage. She is acquainted with the subject from the heart and her gifts and abilities expressed in the written word bring to life the feelings and struggles associated with loss. This book is assured to warm the heart, strengthen the soul, and provide much needed practical suggestions for remarriage. Shirley and Jim masterfully mix the truth of God with the longings of the human heart. This book is certain to bless many.

—Rich Blum, Senior Pastor
Bethel Community Church, Washougal, Washington
bethelcommunitychurch.org

Jim and Shirley have presented a very thorough journey through the deepest part of their hearts in this book. I have known Jim for more than twenty years and Shirley since their dating days. I have witnessed the beautiful thing that God has done in, through, and for them. Honesty and transparency mark the core of this writing as they seek to help others wade through the oftentimes gut-wrenching waters of a great loss. With these tools, their prayer is that others will be able to approach new relationships from a healthy platform, bathed in prayer. To God be all the glory!

—Paul Auble, Senior Pastor
Corbett Community Church, Corbett, Oregon

Shirley Mozena, a national speaker, is the person to write this book. Having suffered the sorrows of being widowed twice, she emerged with depth and character. Having a great present marriage to Jim, they together have facilitated GriefShare for over five years. Want a quick unrealistic sugar stick? This won't be it. It is guaranteed to be a realistic view of not only the joys but also the costs and warning flags of remarriage.

—**Jon Drury,** Pastor
Twenty-one year director of Christian Writers Seminar
Author of *Lord I Feel So Small, BOU Pilot,* over 450 articles

Shirley Mozena knows plenty about the loss of a spouse and what it takes to effectively move through the ensuing grief. I've been down the same path, and she's right. There are reasons, and the right timing, to move ahead with a new marriage, but only after doing some up-front work. This book reveals key issues every couple should talk about before saying "I do" again. As an advocate for marriage and family, I recommend reading the wisdom tucked into these pages. Take Shirley's words to heart as a reminder that happy marriages are not to be entered lightly.

—**Maxine Marsolini**
Author and coach, Rebuilding Families
Host of *Live It Out* blog talk radio

SECOND CHANCE AT LOVE

SECOND CHANCE AT LOVE

A Practical Guide to Remarriage after Loss

Shirley Quiring Mozena

CO-AUTHORED WITH JAMES P. MOZENA

We dedicate this book to the couples all around the world who have lost a spouse through death or divorce. To those who are striving to pursue a new relationship in another committed marriage.

We want to acknowledge the challenges and joys we have experienced from our previous marriages and thank: Bill Rudberg, Blair Graybill, Margi Siberz, and Kathy Mozena. You each have contributed to the foundation we now enjoy.

While marriage is a gift from God, it is only temporary. A vertical relationship with Jesus Christ is the most important relationship we can obtain that is eternal.

May our Lord grant each reader a loving and caring relationship as you pursue a *Second Chance at Love*.

Jim and Shirley Mozena

Contents ✑

Introduction ∽

Are You Ready?

From Shirley

"*I*'m sorry. He's gone," he said gently. Matt was the ICU nurse attending my husband Bill.

Gone? My beloved husband of forty years?

We had celebrated our fortieth anniversary doing what we loved best, exploring the outdoors in beautiful Glacier and Banff National Parks. But a headache that would not go away shortened our trip. Bill had contracted an incessant virus. Eventually, he suffered a stroke and six months after our memorable wedding anniversary trip, I heard those devastating words: "He's gone."

Months passed and I began to learn to live without the man who'd been by my side for forty years. The thought of going on without Bill was like looking down a chasm into a world of nothing but fear and loneliness. I depended on God to get me through this time that was more difficult than any loss I'd ever experienced.

After many lonely months, I longed to share my life with

someone again and joined an online dating site—my nickname was "Loves2dance." A certain guy, whose nickname was "Teacherguy1492," caught my eye. We chatted back and forth through the matching site. When I received an email with the subject line saying, "Would you like to dance?" my heart skipped a beat.

His real name was Blair, and we clicked. When I introduced Blair to my sister, she said, "There's a sweetness about him."

Within six months, we were married. I never dreamed I'd meet and fall in love with someone besides my husband, Bill, but I did! We both marveled that we were a perfect match.

Blair had one more year of teaching before retirement. One evening as we prepared for bed, I noticed his face, shiny with perspiration, had a vacant look. "What's wrong?" I asked.

"I have a headache," he replied. A few moments later he said, "I think you should call an ambulance." At the hospital, I learned it was a brain aneurysm. He never regained consciousness before he died.

I walked through the halls in the hospital and raged silently at God. I didn't understand why this was happening. We'd only had seventeen months of marriage! Couldn't we have more time? I'd already been widowed. Did I have to go through this again?

Though sadness was my partner for months and months, I continued to live. But I began to think recovery would require a new relationship.

Twenty-Six Months Later . . .

"It's over. I can't marry you."

I took the phone away from my ear for a moment in shock and looked at it—the phone, not the voice I heard—as if the phone and not the voice of my fiancé was telling me this. Why hadn't I paid attention to the red flags I saw but ignored? I was lonely. I wanted to be done with the grief and sadness. I needed to go on through my grief, to the other side. It would take work. And tears. And more time.

From Jim

"Her time is coming soon," said Molly shaking her head. She was Kathy's caregiver, giving final instructions for the day.

Though I knew one day death would come to Kathy, I thought, *not now, another day, another time.*

Kathy slept most of the afternoon, her breaths becoming slower and slower. I watched her chest rising slowly with great effort. And then, it was quiet. She didn't take in any more air.

She was now breathing heavenly air. My Kathy was gone.

I carefully closed her eyes, kissed her gently on her lips, and called Father T with the news. Then I called hospice. They needed to come and certify her death. It was 4:20 in the afternoon.

A few months went by. I was so lonely I decided I'd like to meet someone. Surely the company of a woman would remove the sad feelings. I talked to a trusted friend who told me he knew a single woman I might be interested in. I asked her out on a date. I thought I was on my way out of my grief.

Little did I know my grieving had really just begun . . . .

When LaRay and I became engaged, close friends warned me I was moving too quickly. It had only been six months after Kathy died, but I thought I was ready. I wasn't. A few weeks later, we agreed we weren't right for each other and we ended our engagement.

Those are real scenes from each of our lives. Broken engagements and broken hearts. Loss of money and time. Bruised egos. Had we read a book like the one you are going to read, we might have been spared some of that pain. However, even making right choices does not exclude pain. Life brings pain. Guided by the Holy Spirit, Shirley made the choice to marry her second husband. Having been widowed, she experienced a spark of fear that marrying Blair made her vulnerable to another loss, yet the love was worth the loss. Jesus reminded his disciples of life's difficulties when he said: *I have told you these things, so that in me you may have peace. In this world you will have trouble. But take heart! I have overcome the world* (John 16:33 NIV). Life is full of pain, as we have learned through our life experiences. We hope the experiences in this book may help you determine, with the guidance of the Holy Spirit, that you are ready for a new mate after a long-term marriage has ended by death or divorce.

You're working through the grief process and now you'd like to meet someone you might possibly marry. You're an empty nester; you thought you'd be fine as a single person. You may have grandchildren. You may not be retired yet, but you'd like to be in the next few years—and you'd like a spouse to share it with you.

When you were a teenager or young adult in love, you probably didn't think about what it would be like to be married to this person your whole life. But now you know the realities of married life. You may—or may not—be more cautious. And even though you meet a new someone with whom you are head over heels, caution might not be a bad idea. It is our hope this book will open communication more fully between you and a possible lifetime marriage partner.

In the following chapters, we address seven key issues we think deserve your careful consideration before you take that next important step:

- Grief work
- Faith
- Finances
- Blending families
- Sex
- Health
- Politics

We include separate self-assessment questionnaires throughout the chapters to help you determine where you and your potential partner stand on the issues. A comprehensive questionnaire in the appendix will provide all the questions combined for an overall assessment that can illuminate your conversations and the challenges you might encounter in your future together.

Hard as it might be, answer each question at the end of each chapter as honestly as you can. Each of you should take it separately, then share and discuss your answers. Give examples to assist your partner to fully understand why you answered as you did, or provide details that illustrate your point of view.

It is important to compare and discuss your thoughts with each other. Your communication is crucial when considering remarriage. There are no right or wrong answers—just clearly communicated and jointly understood issues that can play a significant role in developing a deep and satisfying marriage. Keep in mind that if you are reluctant to be totally honest in your answers, it might be you aren't ready for another relationship.

As you read through the following chapters, we hope our stories will help you to recover from your grief and then talk with a possible partner about necessary considerations to begin a new chapter in your life.

One last thing. We enjoy all types of music and have found that it enhances life and connects with the soul. To enrich your reading experience, we've shared carefully chosen titles that go along with each chapter's theme. Go online and enjoy the song together to set the stage before you read the chapter. To begin your journey, start with this song: ♪ "What I Did for Love" ♪ Edward Kleban/Marvin Hamlisch.

For the remainder of the book, please listen to the recommended song at the beginning of the chapter.

Part I ⌒

Chapter One ✑

This Wasn't How It Was Supposed to End

♪ "Ain't No Sunshine" ♪
Bill Withers/Keera

From Jim

"*I*'m nearly ready. I'm just going to check my email." Kathy took a short break from packing for a women's retreat to pull up her email. "I've finally gotten a message from Dr. Richardson!" Kathy read the subject line out loud to me. "You've got Idiopathic Pulmonary Fibrosis—IPF."

"What do you think about this, Jim?" she asked, moving away from the computer so I could see what her pulmonologist had written. I read the message: *I've received results from tests performed and can tell you that you have Idiopathic Pulmonary Fibrosis or IPF. I'll be in touch with you when I return from vacation.*

"I'll check on it while you're at the retreat," I told Kathy.

Gradual onset of shortness of breath . . . progressive and irreversible decline in lung function . . . heart failure . . . pulmonary embolism . . . the list went on. The complications of the disease took my breath away. And chilled my soul.

I was angered at the physician's seemingly blasé email. *Going on vacation!* I fumed. I knew I needed to tell Kathy the full truth, yet I dreaded telling her.

Now that I had read the symptoms, it all made sense. No wonder Kathy couldn't push the garden cart anymore! No wonder she got so tired after only a few hours of work.

When Kathy returned from the retreat two days later, I told her what I'd learned about pulmonary fibrosis. The two of us went to the appointment with the pulmonologist two weeks later. We sat wordlessly as the doctor outlined treatment options. There would be medications with troubling side effects and no guarantee of a cure. A possible lung transplant. The treatments were experimental because no one knew what caused her disease.

After our appointment, we drove the thirty-minute ride home. The wind buffeted our car as we drew closer to our home near the Columbia River Gorge. Our emotions were just as turbulent as the wind. We were both shocked beyond words; neither of us could speak.

"Let's make some coffee," I said. "What do you think about the choices the doctor gave us?" I asked as I busied myself with the coffee beans, grinding them and adding them to the coffee pot.

Kathy seemed relatively calm. "I know the Lord knows about all of this. But I'm scared. The docs want to help—but we both know sometimes the treatment is worse than the illness. Remember what Kelly went through." Her cousin Kelly had been so ill from the side effects of chemo that her last months on earth were a nightmare. "I sure as heck don't want to go to Kaiser every single week and wait in line to be poked and prodded. I've read about the side effects of the medicine to prevent rejection if I got a lung transplant—even if I qualify!"

Kathy slammed her hand on the table in frustration. Since she'd been in the medical business for twenty years, she knew first-hand about medical complications. "I'm not anxious to be connected at the hip to the clinic. I don't like how the meds make me feel. Let's just try to enjoy what quality of life I have right now," she said.

"I worry about Cole, though," her voice wavered, "What will happen to my little boy? His mama is gone and soon I'll be gone . . ." She began to sob and didn't finish her words. Cole was our two-year old grandson who lived with us part time. I couldn't help wondering why this had to happen now. Our daughter Kara—she was really my stepdaughter, but I'd helped raise her—had died suddenly of sleep apnea a few months earlier. We'd taken over the care of her only child, Cole, mostly full time while his father was so grief-stricken he was unable to care for him.

"Maybe they're wrong about how long you have . . ." I said with false bravado. "I'll go along with whatever treatment you want"—trying to soften the situation with my support. I didn't admit it to her, but I was afraid. I wasn't ready to let go of my wife. It seemed our troubles were mounting as furiously as the east winds buffeting our house outside.

My consulting business was flourishing, but I began to slow it down. The second year, I sold it so I could be home with Kathy. Later, when she needed twenty-four-hour care, I put my adjunct teaching position at a local college on pause and cared for her full time.

At first the illness wasn't too bad. She still attended church and cooked some of our meals, but gradually she was able to do little but care for her personal needs, like dressing and bathing. Eventually, I helped her with those, too.

And then December before Kathy died, she became very ill. "You're very sick, Kathy. Frankly, I'm not sure you'll make it until January. I'm going to recommend you go on hospice," the pulmonologist said gently. She explained that with hospice, Kathy would receive specialized care because of her life-limiting illness. "They'll be there for you, too, Jim, to advise you with personal care and emotional support."

I was shocked, yet not surprised. Kathy looked twenty years older than she had just six months earlier. This IPF was a terrible, wasting disease.

Kathy fooled us all and rallied. In January, they gave her three more months. Yet each time we visited the doctor, her lungs had deteriorated even more, so her survival was month to month. Since Kathy's comfort was the prime objective, we found hospice to be very helpful. Instead of trying to cure Kathy's illness—which was not curable—they treated Kathy with comfort and pain management. They answered questions we had, gave guidance in care and respite care, visiting our home several times a week.

It might sound grim. Selling a business. Waiting for someone to die. Besides that, I didn't really believe she would die. It didn't seem possible.

I enjoyed doing things for Kathy. The best part about her illness was that she and I communicated like never before. A mentor and close friend visited us weekly. Father T is a retired Episcopal priest, formerly the director of chaplaincy at Good Samaritan Hospital in Portland, and he and I had once worked together. Each time he visited us he gave us an assignment to discuss during the week:

- Share any regrets we'd experienced during our marriage.
- Share what we appreciated about each other.
- Clarify any misunderstandings we'd had.
- Discuss hopes for the future of our children and grandchildren.
- Consider the possibilities of future relationships I might have after she died.

In a sense, this was pre-grief for me and for Kathy. We laughed. We cried. We talked as never before. We knew our time was limited. "I'm sorry I didn't trust you more," Kathy told me, brushing her tears away. Our marriage, especially during the child-raising years, had been tumultuous. We were a blended family, which had presented added challenges.

"I'm sorry we were in the 'crazy cycle' for so long," I said, shaking my head, blowing my nose. Our arguments had seemed to go around and around the same subject. Raising kids in our blended family—her way or my way. I was too hard on her kids. I didn't discipline my own enough. We argued about sex. She said I was never satisfied. I said she was never interested. "You were a good mom to my kids. They knew you loved them—especially Kevin and Bryan. Most of all, Kathy, I wouldn't know Jesus like I do now if you hadn't spoken up."

Friends and family would stop by during the next weeks; but after a while, visiting became too tiring for Kathy. Her world began shrinking to only brief visits with those very close to her—her best friend, her son and stepsons, and of course her beloved grandson Cole.

That unforgettable Monday, July 25, 2011, I knew Kathy's time on earth would not be long. She slept most of the time and took slow breaths. Father T spent the weekend with me, believing Kathy might transition to heaven during that time. But Kathy surprised us. Monday dawned and she was still with us. That morning Father T left for his own home fifty miles away.

Later that morning, Kathy opened her eyes and croaked, "I want a Pepsi."

"A Pepsi?" I asked, surprised because she'd not eaten or desired anything for days. But I hurried to the refrigerator, grabbed the can and stuffed a straw into the opening. "Here we go," I said, holding the beverage for her. She sipped, then stopped to catch her breath.

"Thank you," Kathy said as she laid her head back on the pillow. Then she lifted it up again. "More, please." With a slurp, the can was emptied. She closed her eyes, exhausted from the effort.

Later that morning, Kathy's hospice nurse's aide, Molly, came to bathe and change her linens. She dried Kathy's spindly arms and put fresh pajamas on her after giving her a bath. Molly gently brushed Kathy's freshly shampooed hair and hummed softly to herself as she straightened the light blanket over Kathy's legs and patted the bed.

Though I knew one day death would come to Kathy, I thought, *Not now. Another day, another time . . .*

The black hearse carrying her body wove down the long, curvy driveway. I brushed tears from my eyes and my voice trembled as I said, "Goodbye, Kathy." She was leaving our home for the last time.

Kathy wasn't the first person I'd been with who passed to eternity. I had been with my father when he died and I was thirty years old. I consider it an honor to have been with Kathy and my dad when they made the passage from this earth to the next life.

Two days after Kathy died, I was outside working in my yard. My neighbor to the north stopped her car in the driveway and asked, "How's Kathy?"

"She died on Monday. She seemed very peaceful," I told her.

"Was it in the afternoon?" she asked.

"At 4:20," I answered.

Sarah gasped. "Something strange happened to me on Monday afternoon. You know I mow the south side on Mondays after work. I was out mowing on my lawn tractor. It was noisy, but beyond the mower sound I heard bells ringing. You know, like church bells clanging together in celebration. I heard people cheering like at a sporting event. I heard this *over* the sound of my mower. It was *loud!*"

She paused, taking a breath. "Now that you've told me the time, it makes sense. I think heaven was celebrating Kathy's entry! It was 4:20."

Many people were at Kathy's memorial service to celebrate her life, but we had a special celebration a month after her death—a garden tour of our property. Our place just above the Sandy River Gorge was beautiful that summer with walking paths, a play area for the children, a horseshoe court, flower gardens, and benches where visitors could sit to enjoy the beautiful three acres. We invited people from all over the area to enjoy our gardens. It was even announced on the local radio garden show. After the tour, close friends and family stayed for a dinner outdoors. I know Kathy would have been pleased.

Now I'd done all I could do for Kathy. I had taken care of her during her illness. Had been with her when she died. Had organized a memorial service she would have been proud of and completed the garden tour.

I hiked down to a special place on the Sandy River with my friend Tony and scattered her ashes there. Kathy had asked me to do this. She reasoned that her ashes would blend into the Sandy River that flowed into the Pacific Ocean, evaporate, and turn into clouds that would move back over the mountains as rain and return to the river. "The circle of life," she said.

I grieved for several months, attending a GriefShare class for thirteen weeks and journaling as they recommended. I sorted through Kathy's things and gave most of them away. I cried buckets of tears; and as I said, worked hard at restoring our place, making it beautiful for the garden tour at the end of the summer.

I was so lonely. I'd completed my grief work (or so I thought) and was finally ready to meet someone. The company of a woman would surely remove the lingering sadness. A trusted friend told me he knew a single woman I might be interested in. I asked her out on a date. This was it; I was on my way out of my grief.

Little did I know my grieving had only just begun.

From Shirley

The first twenty years of marriage to Bill had been filled with conflict, and I hadn't been sure if we would make it. But we learned how to live together and communicate with counseling and lots of prayer. And I joined him in his passion for hiking and mountain climbing. My whole life could be compared to those mountain and rock climbs. It was filled with high points akin to sitting atop a mountain after a strenuous climb as well as hard challenges and heartbreak. Sometimes I've cried out, "I can't do this!" But loss has always been interspersed with joy. And there has always been another mountain to conquer.

Some of our hikes rewarded us with stunning views far below. A gleaming river. Steep slopes covered with trees and a buttercup-sprinkled green meadow in the distance. Birdsong that sounded so happy it made me want to sing. Sometimes the hike *was* treacherous and dangerous. You could lose your footing—even your life.

After the first conflicted twenty years, we had another wild twenty-year ride, this time united in climbing mountains, scaling rock walls, and backpacking in the Pacific Northwest.

When Bill turned fifty-one (eleven years before his death), he began to have flu-like symptoms that would not go away. After numerous tests and a bone marrow biopsy, he was diagnosed with chronic lymphocytic leukemia. Though this blood cancer was not acute, the doctor cautioned there was no treatment and at some point Bill's immune system might be compromised. For about six years, there seemed to be little change in Bill's condition until blood tests revealed his white count was rising. Chemotherapy every nine months with few side effects allowed him to continue his job as a manufacturing engineer.

But then, the last summer of Bill's life we took a trip to Banff, and there Bill developed a headache that would not go away. Was this headache a sign that his chronic illness was getting worse?

The next few months were treacherous and hard.

"Ice. Ice!" Bill's frantic voice called me from the bedroom one morning. The pain surges from the shingles of the eye caused my strong mountain man to gasp with the pain. I'd run to his bed and give him an ice pack to cool the agonizing nerve pain. The following days brought on more pain—needle-like pain pricking all over his body. He couldn't formulate his words. His belly ached. There were panic attacks at night.

And then, one evening he had a TIA—a mini stroke. The following afternoon, just before I brought him to the hospital, he had a major stroke. I experienced overwhelming dread. Would I lose Bill? This was far worse than any perilous mountain climb or rappel off a skyscraper-sized rock. How long could my mountain climber husband take these assaults on his body? When tests revealed all four of the major arteries of his brain had been obstructed, the neurologists were dumbfounded. Two days later, a neurosurgeon performed a cerebral angioplasty of his major arteries. This improved his speech and muscle control, and we were grateful to see him rally. But five days later, I received a phone call from ICU telling us to come quickly.

He lay in the dim light with his eyes closed; a tube in his mouth snaking down his windpipe was taped securely to his face. I hated that I couldn't kiss his lips. Beep, beep, beep went the heart monitor. Hiss, sigh, hiss, sigh: the ventilator signaled he couldn't breathe on his own. I sat down beside Bill's bed, feeling the weight of forty years of memories. Joy at the births of our children. Sadness when we lost our baby girl. Memories of beautiful hikes and climbs. And terrible memories—of our battles early in our marriage and later of battles of Bill's illness.

I sang songs I knew would encourage him: *When peace, like a river, attendeth my way . . .*

Our children took turns sitting on the opposite side of his bed. Each told him how much they loved him. "We're right here," they said. Somehow we knew it would be the last time we would talk to him this side of heaven.

At 3:00 a.m. I looked at his dear face that seemed to be turning gray. The nurse said, "He's gone." And the family he loved so much had to figure out how to live without his commanding presence.

I don't know how we got home. We celebrated Bill's life with a beautiful graveside and memorial service, but the world was strange. Different. Cold.

Months passed and I began to learn to live without the man who'd been by my side for forty years. Going on without Bill was like looking down a long hallway with no end in sight. A life without my hero and father of my children. I depended on God to get me through this loss, greater than any loss I'd ever experienced. I paced the hall at night. I couldn't sleep. My Bible was the only book I really wanted to read. I was and am an avid reader, but fiction just didn't delight or stimulate me as it usually had. My situation was as stark as any tragic novel, and the reality of my life prevented any escape into fiction. Though it helped to be around other people, I couldn't be with them all the time. What did help was prayer, since I knew God was available any time.

I relived those harrowing months when Bill was so sick. I wept for him—and for me.

During those sleepless nights, I would remember Bible verses that I'd memorized as a young child. They reminded me I was in "the valley of the shadow of death." I was comforted that Bill was "dwelling in the house of the Lord." There were many verses that spoke to me of God's ever presence and how much he loved me and wanted my broken heart to be healed. But I tried other coping strategies. I worked on the house that needed a new face. I pushed myself to keep busy by painting the living areas. I changed our bedroom into *my* bedroom, remodeled the bathrooms. My financial situation forced me to find a new job; on that job I learned completely new knowledge and skills. I continued to visit the gym three times a week, hiked regularly with female friends. Keeping my body in shape was important to me—I figured I'd need good health to take care of myself now that I was alone.

My grandchildren gave me comfort. They stayed overnight so their parents could have breaks with time by themselves. My ninety-year-old mother lived in an assisted living community in a city nearby and I made regular visits with her. She, too, reminded me of how much God loved me. She even advised, "Use the modern way—the computer—to meet someone." At church the music soothed my soul, and I was reminded of God's faithfulness, of how much God loved me. After a few months, I returned to singing on my church worship team. I even joined my single girlfriends in some Christian singles dances and had fun pushing myself into areas I wasn't comfortable with—I had never danced real dance steps until then.

After two years, I yearned to share my life with someone. Dancing at those singles dances with a man's arm around me felt so comfortable. I missed preparing meals for my husband and hearing his positive remarks about my cooking. I'd enjoyed being married and wondered if it might happen again. Very early in my widowhood, I remembered a colleague at work telling me, "You might not want to think about it now, but God might bring another man into your life. Perhaps even get married." I laughed out loud because it was beyond my realm of consideration, yet a spark of hope grew as time passed. In my prayer times, I begged God to show me if I should pursue looking for someone to marry. Though I had never dreamed I could want someone else, I began exploring online options, joined a dating site, and studied the possible matches the site sent me.

But it was a conversation with a friend that I believe revealed God's choice for me. This friend recommended I try a *different* matching site that her sister had used—who was now happily married to someone she met at that particular site. After that conversation, she even called me the next day to make sure I would try the site.

I enrolled, and three days later, Blair popped into my matches. He was a widower who shared my belief system. I sensed the Holy Spirit guided me, and circumstances confirmed that belief. Our first meeting was a long phone conversation through which we connected in many ways. We agreed to meet face to face for dinner and stayed until the restaurant closed. As we walked to our separate cars, he asked me for another date the following evening, and after that we either met or spoke by phone daily. Though we were both working full time, we sensed that spending time with each other was very important.

Within six months, Blair and I were married. We both marveled that we were a perfect match.

A few months after our wedding, Blair took a leave of absence for us to travel together to beautiful South Africa. We went on safari and stayed at a swanky resort in the middle of the African bush. I convinced Blair to climb Table Mountain in the hot African sun. It was a heady experience, walking on the flat green summit, viewing beautiful Cape Town and the harbor far below. For six weeks, we enjoyed the summertime climate south of the equator.

In late December, we returned to our winter and Blair resumed his teaching position. It was to be his last year before retirement. One month later, as we prepared for bed, I noticed his face had a vacant look and was shiny with perspiration. "What's wrong?" I asked.

"I have a headache," he replied. A few moments later he said, "I think you should call an ambulance." At the hospital, I learned a brain aneurysm had killed him.

I walked through the halls in the hospital and raged silently at God. I didn't understand why this was happening. We'd only had seventeen months of marriage! Couldn't we have more time? I'd already been widowed once. Did I have to go through that again?

Those first few months after Blair's sudden death, my sadness reminded me of him everywhere I drove. Once I impulsively stopped at a salon and asked for a pedicure. The warm bubbling foot bath was pleasant, and while I enjoyed a fresh bright red polish for my toes, it distracted me only for a time.

Other distractions didn't work either. I couldn't watch movies. I couldn't read fiction. The only thing that helped was reading my Bible, especially the Psalms that soothed my wounded soul. I was reminded in grief class that I needed to go on through my grief to the other side. It would take work, such as going through Blair's clothing, the many collections of his hobbies, his letters, and classroom notes he'd carefully kept. I journaled. I attended GriefShare. It took tears. Time. Work.

Fast forward two years. I thought I was ready for a new relationship. I even wrote a book that was nearly complete when I met someone who was raised in the same town as Blair in Southern California. But the similarity ended there. We met on the same internet site where Blair and I had met. Ron seemed like a decent guy. He didn't have the education my previous mates had and instead educated himself by reading. He loved his family. He talked about his children and the excitement of a new grandbaby soon to enter the family. During long phone conversations, he told me about his conversion and faith in Christ and about the church where he was a member. After several phone conversations, he suggested we meet face to face. Could we meet at my church and attend service together? He would stay with his daughter, who lived nearby, and we could meet face to face and get to know each other. I agreed, and our first meeting went very well. We communicated easily and there was chemistry too.

True, his finances were a bit rocky: he'd been divorced twice and those facts bothered me, yet I reasoned those divorces took place before he became a Christian and things would be different now. Why did I ignore the other red flags? I was lonely. I missed the companionship of a man. And most of all, I stubbornly ignored my unease and accepted his proposal of marriage—after all, it had been the same length of time between the death of my first husband, Bill, and my engagement to Blair. I should have listened to family members who cautioned me I was moving too fast. I should not have pushed doubting thoughts away. Doubts that I believe came from the Holy Spirit. Instead, I allowed my hope and strength to come from a man who might make me feel better. Together Ron and I prayed regularly to discern God's will for our marriage. That prayer was answered in a way I didn't expect. Our engagement ended after the phone call Ron made five weeks before our wedding.

We both had experienced the jarring loss of our spouses. Sometimes we moved too quickly to soothe that terrible loss. We learned it takes more than time or another person to heal the hurt of grief and loss. After all, grief is life, and that's what we'll discuss in the next chapter.

Chapter Two ∽

Grief Is Life!

♪ "What a Wonderful World" ♪
Bob Thiele/George David Weiss

There is grief, not just in death or divorce, but in everyday life. Some losses are small; I am sad when we reach summer solstice which means our long days filled with light will be lessening each day. There are greater losses, perhaps an empty nest—children who depended on us now are on their own. When we turn the calendar page, we are aware time is moving forward and our days on earth are fewer.

There are other losses that bring grief: loss of health, loss of identity through retirement, loss of youth, loss of memory, loss of physical capabilities, loss of a family home, loss of a driver's license because of physical limitations. The list can go on and on.

You've probably realized that every day means there are fewer tomorrows. So you should think carefully through whatever time God has planned for you. Will you marry again? Do you want to be married? You need to be sure you've worked through your grief before you even think about marrying again.

What is the work of grief?

"Grief work" is a process each of us must go through when we have significant loss, and for the topic of this book, that means either the death of a loved spouse or death of a marriage through divorce. We experience many losses in our lifetime. Loss of job, loss of health, retirement, serious illness, moving out of a home after a long period of time, broken friendships—but until we each experienced the death of our previous spouses, we both realized there's no preparation for it. But you can take steps after the loss. Following are the steps involved with grief work that need to be taken in order to be confident you are ready for another relationship.

From Shirley

Lean in to your grief. I've hiked many trails in the Pacific Northwest. One is Dog Mountain. It's a strenuous climb high above the Columbia River Gorge, rewarding me with a fabulous view at the top. Wildflowers dot the meadows along the steep trail, and in May the sunny yellow Balsam Root drench the slopes with their color as I trudge along. The Columbia River sparkles far below. Most often, there is a stiff wind on the upper portion that gouges the rocky path up and up. I found it helped to l-e-a-n into the wind as I plodded up the trail. If I stand up straight, it causes instability. I might lose my footing with a dangerous edge on one side. It's far better to lean.

Just as I learned to lean in to the blustery, steep trail, you must lean in to your grief. Face the loss and don't be afraid of the grief. The emotions of grief won't kill you; they will only make you stronger when the next steep trail of grief hits you. It will take strength and a mind-set to push yourself, but it will help you move through your grief.

Cry out to God. Share your honest feelings. You don't have to fear what he thinks. He loves you and is right there with you as you cry to him. Be honest—he can take it. Scripture tells us God . . . *collected all my tears in your bottle/You have recorded each one in your book* (Psalm 56:8 NLT). One woman said she went up to the third floor of her house, got on the treadmill, and screamed out to God in her grief. She knew no one but God would hear her. You might go out in nature—even out your front door. God is ever-present even though we don't feel like he is—talk to him like he is there. Ask a godly friend or pastor to pray with or for you.

We both took refuge in prayer and reading God's Word during our mourning period, during our courtship, and in our daily life. It helps . . . *but those who hope in the LORD will renew their strength* (Isaiah 40:31 NIV). We've both discovered that depending on the promises of God is a daily, deliberate choice. We believe he will heal your broken heart because he cares. It may sound simple but keep trusting and don't quit.

Journal your grief. You do not have to be a writer to journal. Record your emotions and memories in a notebook. Here are some writing prompts to help you journal:

- What are hopes and dreams you had for the future that are no longer possible?
- What are the most significant losses you have experienced because of this death? You may be surprised.
- What are some of your secondary losses, such as: having a person take out the trash, having the car serviced, having the lawn mowed, having tax prepared, and having repairs done around the house?
- What do you wish you'd asked your spouse that you cannot ask now?
- Are you able to forgive your spouse for things he or she did to contribute to the death of your marriage?
- Even if you were happily married, are there things you need to forgive? Write down the answers to those questions and

concerns. Ask God to help you forgive. Then destroy the paper.

- What do you miss most about your spouse? What do you miss least?
- What kind of legacy will you pass on to the younger people in your family now that your spouse is no longer here on earth?
- What is your role in encouraging your grandchildren in their family heritage and to convey your loved one's hopes and desires for them?

This is for you alone; reread your entries. Are you moving forward through the grief? Do you break down and cry every time you think about your loved one? Are you able to talk about your loss without crying? When you look back at your loss, are you grateful for the memories? Take inventory of the ways God is blessing you during your grief.

Retrace your past. Look at photos, read letters, cards. If you are able, drive by places you lived with your spouse. In your journal describe hopes and dreams you had for the future that are no longer possible, or never happened. Both of us sorted through files—especially medical files once the medical bills and insurance was paid, then shredded the thick files. They were no longer necessary. I cried as I shredded them, talking out loud as if to my husband: "I'm so sorry." Another form of retracing the past. With my second husband and our marriage only lasting seventeen months, I typed out all our notes to each other and emails we wrote back and forth. It helped me remember those times, and it verified we did have a life together.

Examine various events associated with your marriage. Think back on anniversaries of significant events in your courtship and your wedding. Birthdays. Children's births. Anniversaries of death or divorce. Memorable holidays. Your honeymoon. Travels.

Some may have been pleasant and wonderful, but most likely there were some difficult vacations or lifetime events during your marriage. I found writing the difficult events down helped me process them. Then I often threw the writings away. For several months, I watched the slide show we played at my husband's memorial service. It was healing as I watched and laughed and cried.

Face the loss. Facing grief is scary, and we might be afraid the grief could kill us, or at least overwhelm us. We can tell you it won't. Retrace past experiences with your loved one. Perhaps re-visiting a favorite restaurant, or listening to music you enjoyed together. Shirley retraced hikes she'd taken with her husband in the past.

Think back to a time when you've had to do physical therapy for an injury or surgery. It was difficult. Painful, but necessary for your healing. That is facing your loss.

Here are questions to ask yourself to help you face the loss:

- What objects, pictures, or places make you think of your spouse?
- Which restaurants did you frequently visit with your late spouse?
- What music brings good memories about your spouse?

Examine previous losses. Do you find yourself crying about events long past? List your losses. It could be a miscarriage, the death of a friend, breaking up with another lover before your marriage, the loss of a pet. Ask the Holy Spirit to reveal them. Talk it over with a counselor or trusted friend. Write them down.

I was asked to list my losses during one of my grief classes. "Perhaps you haven't fully grieved some of them," the facilitator stated. After listing the losses, the one that stood out was the loss of my baby girl named Carrie Lynn. My heart was still very deeply wounded by the shame and regret surrounding her inexplicable death in my womb. After I realized I hadn't completed grief work,

I wrote Carrie a letter. I told her I was sorry I never got to see or touch her. I told her I was sorry I wasn't more proactive in taking care of her precious body with a proper burial. I faced the fact I didn't know what the hospital did with her body—and I acknowledged my guilt for not knowing. I confessed to God that I had overreacted in my hurt. He forgave me. Now I needed to forgive myself. My heart began to hurt less.

Although this damage to my heart wasn't part of any relationship trauma, the sorrow of it would still have affected any new relationship I started with a man. A whole heart is important to a healthy relationship, and this includes healing from losses of all kinds.

Take action. If you've had a difficult time attending worship services since your loss, go and do it. You'll be stronger for it. The first time you attend a worship service after a long period of time, come after the service has begun to avoid uncomfortable encounters with people who care about you, but you just don't want to break down. Sit in a different place than you did with your loved one. If you cannot attend the church you've belonged to for a long time, find another place to worship.

Take yourself out to a nice restaurant alone. Enjoy the freedom to choose where to go, where to sit, and when you want to leave. I found release in discovering I enjoyed my own company and just observing other people.

Listen to your loved one's memorial service. Both of us listened to them with family members and when we met, listened to our late spouses' services together. Listening several times is helpful.

Go through your mate's clothing. Keep what you cannot part with and put them in a memory box along with other mementos of your spouse and give the other items to charity or to family members who might want them.

Examine yourself.

- Are you comfortable being with just yourself, or do you have to always be with someone? If you are comfortable, that indicates you may be ready for a new relationship. Needing to always be with someone indicates you have some work to do.
- Do you tear up every time you think of your loss?
- Do you treat your loss as though it happened only weeks ago? Answering yes indicates you have more grief work to do.
- Are you willing to be alone/not marry for the rest of your life? If you answer yes, this indicates you are prepared to face life alone or with a partner. Sounds like you're ready. But if you are unable to do some or all these things, you may not be ready for a new relationship.

Grief is not linear. It isn't likely you will take "X" number of steps and your grief will be complete. There is an ebb and flow to grief and sadness, and it doesn't flow precisely from one stage to the next.

Jim remembers an invasion of sadness while teaching his business class: "How do you balance career and home life?" a female student asked.

"I thought about her question and began to answer, but I was distracted by something else," he told me. *Her voice sounded just like Kathy's!* "I tried to focus back on the question, but I couldn't. I had a huge lump in my throat that wouldn't go away. Tears formed in my eyes as I attempted to speak.

"Let's take a short break and we'll talk about it when you come back." I was ambushed by grief. After the break, I was able to compose myself and continue the class, but I'll never forget the helpless feelings of grief that overwhelmed me at that moment.

There are other things that might trigger grief when you think you're doing fine: walking through the grocery store and seeing your person's favorite brand of tea; you realize you don't need to buy it anymore.

Shirley remembers a scene in her home one summer afternoon:

"I came into the house from the bright sunshine. My eyes were adjusting to the dimness in the cool house when I glanced up—and there in the dining room stood Blair. He was his neat self, in his short-sleeved shirt. *You didn't die!* I thought. *Oh, I missed you so much.* But then reality struck. I blinked and he was gone . . ."

When married to your previous spouse, you assimilated some of your spouse's taste in decor, food, music. While you adjust to your new normal, you may develop new skills, or new hobbies not encountered in your previous life. Now's your chance to try something new. To be yourself in a new way—not who you think you should be for someone else. This is an important process of moving through grief.

You will have interruptions of great sadness, but more and more you will remember with joy what you had. Grief is the price of love and grief work is the price of healing. The cost is worth it to be healed and to love again. It isn't fair to your future mate if you have not done all the work in your grief. To love again, you need to pay the emotional cost—doing the above and more. Although there's no magic formula or exact number of steps, there is a process. You must move *through*—not *around*—the grief to get to the other side.

We really enjoyed writing this chapter, reminiscing our first date and what ensued . . .

Don't forget to listen to the song to set the stage for our next subject.

Chapter Three ✑

How Do We Meet?

♪ "The First Time Ever I Saw Your Face" ♪
Ewan McColl

From Shirley

I was a bit late as I drove into the crowded parking lot. Meeting someone for the first time is always an adventure. I braced myself for the disappointment I'd experienced so many times. But then I found myself thinking optimistically, imagining that things would be different this time. The sun peeked through the clouds as I stepped past outdoor tables scattered with people. I glanced inside. Nearby stood a trim man dressed in jeans and polo shirt and with a full head of salt-and-pepper hair. His back was to me as he surveyed the crowded lunchtime group.

"Are you Jim?"

He turned to me, friendly blue eyes framed by wire-rimmed square glasses. He flipped his laptop open, looked at my profile photo on the screen and said, "You must be Shirley."

Our coffee cups long drained, we got up to leave. Jim walked me into the parking lot. "I like your car. It says something about you. And you like red!"

"I do." We said goodbye and Jim gave me a sideways hug. He pulled away, slowly, as though he didn't want to let go. I didn't want him to, either.

From Jim

I arrived early and found a table to observe the main entrance to the coffee shop. As I waited, the minutes seemed like hours. Then it was 12:35. There she was. Wow! She looked just like her photo on the website. Blonde hair, and with her arresting blue eyes I was immediately attracted. Slender, in dressy slacks and a sleeveless blouse, she confidently walked into the shop.

I felt an instant connection. It was easy to converse with her. She was enthusiastic, attractive and athletic, with a wonderful laugh. *Boy, this is looking good.*

"What's the name of your book?" I asked.

"*Second Chances at Life and Love, With Hope,*" she said.

I promptly opened my computer and ordered it. I said, "I've got Amazon prime, so I'll get this in two days!" She had a big smile on her face when I did that. *Score for me!*

The moments turned into two hours. I asked, "Would you like to meet again? I'd enjoy going to a worship service with you."

"I would like that," she said with a smile. "I won't be going to my own church this Sunday, but if you don't mind visiting a different one with me . . ."

"Great! How about I come to your house—if you feel comfortable my coming there—we could have coffee and go to church from there?"

"I'll have the coffee on!"

Reluctant to say goodbye, I said, "I'll walk you to your car." Her red Volkswagen said a lot to me. Sporty. Bold, yet feminine.

I drove off feeling very good and wondered, *is she the one?* I was anxious to get her book to learn more about her.

Later that evening, I followed up with an email telling her how much I enjoyed our date. I gave her more information about my extended family.

I prayed and hoped this would be the start to a journey of love and happiness.

So how did we find each other? There are many places to meet someone special you may want to spend your life with, more avenues to meet than ever before. We'll tell you the way we met in a moment. Here are some suggestions:

- Community college class
- Church, or church singles group
- Outings sponsored by your city or county parks and recreation
- Hiking or bike club
- Christian singles dance or community contra dances
- Square dancing; often held in community halls or grange halls
- Introduction by a trusted friend to someone they think would be a good match
- Match service

Don't be cheap: there are free ones, but we recommend you put some skin in the game. Shirley had found success with Match.com, and E-Harmony worked for both of us.

We are often asked how we met. When we answer it was through an online matching service most people are surprised. "Really?" they ask, as if it is not possible. In many ways, a matching site opens your world. Most matching services ask you to list your preferences such as church affiliation and political party, as well as marriage status (widowed or divorced). To my surprise, there were people who put "separated"—an immediate red flag for me!

Some people are afraid to "put themselves out there" on the internet and that's understandable. Keep in mind, the sites are protected. Your communication is through the matching site, not your own email. You can even use a different name until you decide you want to reveal it to a possible match. There are unscrupulous people who will lie to promote themselves, for example, posting ten-year-old photos of themselves. That's human nature; you must judge by what you read and what you ask in communicating with the potential person you want to meet.

Face-to-face meetings are important as well. The connection might be good via phone or email, but there's nothing like a live encounter. Non-verbal communication can tell you a lot.

For your first live introduction, we recommend you meet at a public place. Drive your own car to meet. This is your first meeting and you may never see them again. A cautionary note to women especially: let a friend know you are meeting this person and where the meeting will take place.

Shirley had quite a few dates that were fizzles. Emailing the person after the meeting is quite simple, and if you don't think you're a match, be honest and say just that. It doesn't have to be dramatic. Honesty is the best policy as Jim's first criterion for a good relationship reflects.

From Shirley

After two years of widowhood, I met my second husband on Match.com. If we hadn't met online, we wouldn't have connected. He lived on the east side of town, attended a different church denomination, moved in different circles. At our first meeting online, we connected immediately. We were transparent with each other, with full information about ourselves. I networked him and quickly knew he was who he said he was; most information about anyone is available by typing their name into a search engine.

We met face-to-face for dinner, found we really enjoyed each other's company, and talked nonstop. Our dinner date lasted until the restaurant closed for the night. Within a month, we were engaged with a ring and a wedding date. That might sound sudden, but keep in mind we were in our sixties. We each came from enduring marriages of more than thirty years. Although I had grieved for nearly two years, the moment we met the angst of my loss scuttled away like dried leaves blown about on a windy day.

It's important to accept your aloneness as reality. Another person cannot replace a loved one. After accepting death or divorce, there are many steps of grief you need to take, including the reality you may not meet another person to marry. This is a vital step before looking into meeting someone new.

Blair and I married six months after we met. I never dreamed I'd love someone as much as my husband Bill, but I did! We marveled that we were a perfect match in so many ways. After seventeen months of marriage, we were planning a two-year celebration of our first dinner date at the same restaurant where we'd met earlier, but we never celebrated that date.

As I shared in chapter 1, Blair died suddenly of a brain aneurysm. After he died so suddenly, I was choked with grief everywhere I turned. I traveled to get away from the reminder I was living in my beautiful home without my beloved. I journaled. I cried. I relived wonderful memories.

I vividly remember one Sunday morning I was headed upstairs to get ready for church and the reality of my loss hit me like the rush of a sneaker wave at the beach. It hit me. He was gone! I collapsed on the stairway, not knowing if I could go on. I pushed myself to get ready, but as the water in the shower drenched me, I didn't know if I would recover. In my nakedness I cried out to God to help me. I calmed down after that episode, but the fierceness of my loss is seared in my memory of those early days of loss. I attended grief classes for nearly two years.

Just like after my first husband Bill died, I thought I was ready to meet someone new following Blair's death. Looking back, I paid more attention to the timeline (it had been two years between the death and meeting of someone new) than if I was emotionally ready to meet someone new; that is why I went back to the same website to meet someone. I did, and coincidently Ron was even from Blair's hometown.

Five weeks before the wedding was scheduled, Ron ended our engagement abruptly. I could hardly believe that only earlier that day, Ron had sent loving texts only to be cold and distant later that evening when he made that fateful call. I had put money down on a house we would buy together and because of this abrupt ending of our engagement, it was necessary for me to call the realtor and explain what happened. The earnest money I'd put down was lost because the cancelation was one day too late.

I even had to cancel the reservation we'd made for our honeymoon that was also in my name. It was humiliating. I was also heartbroken. I wanted our relationship to work. I didn't want to be alone. But God taught me so much through that broken engagement that I can now share with you.

From Jim

My first attempt at meeting someone was a flop. A trusted friend introduced me to a woman near my age who attended his church. Sounds good, doesn't it? True, she was fairly attractive and a believer in Christ, but quite different from me. I didn't experience the pizazz I felt when my wife Kathy and I met, and for sure, after meeting Shirley later the feelings and chemistry didn't compare with this woman. She resisted any kind of physical touch, including holding hands.

I had been widowed only six months when we met, and we were soon engaged. She and I were not a good match in many ways. She told me several times she felt no chemistry toward me. Her adult son, in his late twenties, lived with her, and it seemed to me he took over her home—playing acid hard rock music, dominating conversations when I visited at her home, and being sporadically unemployed. In my previous marriages, we had encountered a lot of problems and I thought that's what marriage was, working through one problem after another. We were mismatched from the start, and I ignored these red flags. Yet it was more than that. I was not ready to be involved with someone else. I needed to work through my grief. It was too soon and I was not emotionally healthy. I share this experience in the previous chapter.

It is very important to make sure you are looking for someone not only to replace your deceased or missing spouse because of loneliness, but also because you believe you are ready to move forward. When your loneliness is coupled with the desire to be with a person of the opposite sex, it can be an indication that you may need to continue to work through your grief.

I realized I needed to find contentment in my single state and face the fact I might never meet another woman to marry. I began to enjoy my life the way it was—be involved with my grandchildren and kids. If and when I did find a mate, I needed to be satisfied with my life as it had become—as a single man.

More time passed, and I thought I'd worked through my grief. I jumped into a new relationship. This woman was not even a Christian, but I convinced myself I could lead her to Christ. My pastor, also a good friend, said bluntly, "Jim, aren't you 'missionary dating?'" This woman stated several times she didn't want to marry again, and I was looking for a lifetime partner to marry. I realized I was wanting a partner for the wrong reasons, and over dessert while at a restaurant one evening I stated, "I don't feel like our relationship is going anywhere!" She was very quiet after that as if she felt the same way yet seemed to enjoy the benefits of being with someone. I ended the relationship after that evening.

Still lonely after completing what I thought was plenty of grief work, I renewed my quest to find a wife. This time I prayed. I asked God to bring the right person into my life, not to replace Kathy to relieve my terrible loneliness, but to find a soulmate at *this* time in my life. I did what grief experts recommend: grief work.

I worked through my grief several ways. I continued upkeep on my property: the three acres needed constant attention and the physical work was a good antidote to my loss. I also taught part-time business classes at a local community college. This kept me in the loop with other professionals, and the students stimulated thought.

I enjoyed running along the hills and valleys of the Columbia River Gorge right outside my door, and I regularly took personal retreats in the mountains nearby. Leaving my computer and phone at home, bringing only my Bible, I would pour out my desires to God, asking him to heal my broken heart. I read the Bible, took notes, and journaled. Those retreats settled my soul and drew me closer to God.

And then I believed I was ready to meet someone. I wasn't as desperate to meet a woman as I had been previously. Now I was more focused on finding someone who shared the same lifetime goals and values that I did. I was not willing to compromise on them.

For the next several months, I spent a lot of time in prayer, begging God to reveal his will for me. I read and reread Psalm 119, *I seek you with all my heart* rang through my mind as I ran the mountain roads near my home. *Teach me, LORD, the way of your decrees . . . you have given me hope* (Psalm 119:10, 33 NIV).

At last, I believed I was ready and devised a plan. I believed the Holy Spirit revealed that plan to me through those prayers and reading: first, find a different church that was larger than the one

I'd been a member of for many years. Possibly I'd meet someone in their singles groups. My first venture was a total washout. I felt very out of place and embarrassed to be primarily searching for a woman—or even a date!

Second part of the plan: join an online dating service. I found one advertising a Labor Day Special. After loading photos of myself, I took their personality test. All this was time-consuming, but I reminded myself it'd be worth it.

I nearly canceled the subscription the next day—call it "buyer's remorse." Then someone popped up on my matches who caught my eye. To be honest, there were three. I emailed the women and asked if they'd be willing to meet face-to-face. Two responded. One of them was Shirley and we agreed to meet for coffee the following day. I prayed, asking God to guide our meeting.

From Shirley

More than a year had passed since my breakup with Ron. There was contentment in my life without the anxiety or need to repair my heart. Instead of scrolling through a matching website, I did a lot more praying and asking God to bring a new man into my life. There was peace. I was reminded *The Lord is my shepherd, I have all that I need* (Psalm 23:1 NLT). I learned to be satisfied in my singleness. I was reminded, *For I have learned to be content with whatever I have. I know how to live on almost nothing or with everything* (Philippians 4:11–12 NLT). I hoped I'd marry again, but I was now willing to remain single if that was God's will for me.

I joined a new dating site, taking a long personality quiz about what I wanted for my future. As I sat down in my morning room to read my Bible and devotional, I wondered about E-Harmony, the service I'd recently joined. *If this doesn't work, Lord, I won't do any more searching,* I prayed. My future match would not come about by my manipulating someone into being the right person.

You will just have to drop him in my lap! And Lord, I thought with a smile, *would you make him crazy about me—someone who even loves You more than I do?* Leaving it in his hands, I felt settled. The new dating service sent me photos and profiles of men, and one bright Sunday morning, a new guy came into view. Five-foot-ten, he appeared to be a widower, though I wasn't positive. He lived across the river in the Columbia River Gorge, and he was cute. He talked about the grandson of his deceased daughter that he loved so much. He openly talked of his faith. Jim mentioned an older Christian man who was a mentor to him. He spoke of his desire to be an influence of faith to friends and family. He talked about his interest to keep his body in shape by regularly running the hills near his home. Most of all, Jim was a strong, committed Christian who was obviously not ashamed of his faith.

The matching service asked, "What makes a relationship?" and Jim answered:

1. Honesty
2. Financial security
3. Affection in touch and words
4. Love of family and acceptance of partner's family

After several question exchanges, he sent me a message. "Would you like to meet for coffee?"

"Sure," I responded. "Let's keep emailing." We exchanged our personal email addresses and continued to reveal more of ourselves to each other. He told me his last name and I Googled him, confirming that the resume he sent me was very similar. This guy was thorough! There didn't seem to be any secrets.

Our meeting was timely. Although earlier we seemed almost desperate to meet someone to marry, this time we were spiritually ready. Shirley's engagement breakup taught her to find her comfort and satisfaction in deepening her relationship with God, not another man. Jim realized he was searching for a relationship before his heart was healed. Each were content to remain single if that was God's will.

Be sure to:

- Use a reputable matching site. Be aware there are people who might try to deceive you. Use discretion when meeting someone. Let a friend know what you're doing and where you are meeting.
- Sometimes a trusted friend will introduce you to someone they know and trust. Usually that is reliable, though as Jim found, may not always be the right match.
- Have a trusted friend or prayer partner you can consult with—often they can see and discern red flags you don't see. Be open to listen to them if they express concerns.

Now that you are ready to meet someone—or you've met the one you want to consider as a lifelong partner—we encourage you to allow the Holy Spirit to guide you in your search. The Holy Spirit usually speaks in a quiet, internal voice during your prayer and Bible reading. Be very aware of it and don't discount that quiet voice. Keep in mind God only wants the very best for you. Be intentional in prayer, asking God to reveal to you any red flags and checks in your spirit when you meet.

As we move on to Part 2, you will begin to navigate the trail to remarriage. There are some issues you need to take into account before making a commitment with a potential mate. We discussed different ways to meet, whether it was taking a class, attending a church singles group, joining outings through your parks and recreation community program, joining a hiking or bike club, or—like we did—joining an online matching service. We recommend you take your time in a new relationship and not move too fast. There can be disastrous results.

Don't forget to listen to the chapter's theme song!

Part II ❧

Chapter Four ∽

Moving Too Fast?

♪ "Breaking Up is Hard to Do" ♪
Neil Sedaka

"*I* really enjoyed getting to know you. . .would you like to get together again?" Ron asked in his rumbling deep voice. Ron lived four hours away. It was our first face-to-face meeting, and I liked what I saw. More than six feet tall, he was a former Marine with short-cropped hair. We had shared stories about our past lives. He attended high school in Southern California where he lived until he was an adult. He loved football and played on the school team—the same high school in Southern California that Blair attended. *Was it as a sign we were meant to be?* I wanted it to be so.

"I joined the Marine Corps right after high school," he told me. "Got shipped to Vietnam shortly after basic training."

He appeared in good physical condition and told me he worked out nearly every day at the gym. Proudly, he displayed an American flag on his white truck.

"Sure," I said. I was responding to his invitation as my stomach took a dip with excitement. We made the most of the two days he stayed in the area, attending a worship service at my church, eating several meals together, and even taking a short hike. We talked easily together and were delighted we had similar thoughts about our families, politics and, especially, our Christian beliefs.

"I was thinking maybe you could drive out here. Meet some of my family; I could show you around town. I've got an extra bedroom you can use while you're here."

"I think that might be okay," I said. Inside, my stomach lurched. *This didn't feel right. Was this appropriate to stay in his home?* We didn't know each other that well. Quickly I called two friends whose opinions I valued. I asked them what they thought of my staying at Ron's house in his guest room. One said she thought it would be fine. The other expressed concern. She quizzed me with questions. Do you know him well enough to stay in his home? What does it look like to others, like his family or neighbors? Do you think that looks right even though I know you don't plan to sleep with him? After thinking and praying about it, I made a reservation at a nearby motel and felt better.

Two days later, I drove east to Ron's town for our visit. Although I was excited to get to know this man even more, I was nervous. I wasn't sure about his not having a problem with my staying at his home when we hardly knew each other. I wished he'd wanted to protect me more and made arrangements for me to stay someplace else.

I had always enjoyed the drive through the beautiful ninety-mile canyon known as the Columbia River Gorge. The stunning views entertain visitors and residents alike. Multiple waterfalls— and the crown jewel, Multnomah Falls—are right outside your car window.

Snow-covered Mount Hood looms into view, so close to the highway. And then, at about ninety miles from Portland, there's a stark change. Instead of steep cliffs and evergreens interspersed with waterfalls, there are large, brown, rolling hills. Atop the tall hills are modern-day metal windmills slowly turning to produce energy. The four hours raced by as I listened to my favorite music on the radio and enjoyed the scenery.

My navigation system chimed directions as I drove down the hill into the small, Eastern Oregon town. Our plans were for me to stop by Ron's house before I checked into my room at the motel. We would go out to dinner and I'd meet Ron's son and daughter-in-law that evening.

I drove down the streets surrounded by spindly bare trees. They looked lonely, lining the streets. I glanced at the patches of snow in the brownish grass. It was a cold and blustery December, two days before Christmas. I pulled into a small neighborhood clustered with all styles of homes. I saw double-wide mobile homes, a few ranch style "stick built" homes, and some manufactured homes. To my right as I rounded the curve, I spied an aqua-colored dou-ble-wide mobile home. "Arrived," my phone announced. I was at Ron's. I was surprised at the modesty of his home. *Whoa! This was not what I expected.* Ron had had a good job and it seemed he should have been better established at his age. I didn't want to be judgmental, but finances are a very real and practical consideration when choosing a partner.

Ron was waiting for me, walked out to greet me and wrapped me in a warm hug. "This is it," he said. We walked into the house that was simple but neat. "Would you like some coffee?"

"Sure."

It was good to get out of the car and stretch my legs. We sipped coffee and Ron showed me photographs of his wedding to his late wife, Marie. We talked more about his past life and their relation-ship. She had died of cancer and the end of her life was horrific. Almost as an afterthought, he told me, "She asked me to move out after she found out she had cancer."

"Why?" I quizzed. Inwardly I wondered, *this doesn't seem right. When Bill was so sick, he wanted me nearby all the time.*

"I dunno. I think she thought I irritated her and she'd heal better without me bothering her." I pondered this information that seemed wrong.

He showed me around his home. Neat and clean as a pin. Photos of his children peppered the hallway. He stopped at his desk and pulled a well-used worn ledger out of the center drawer. All his monthly expenditures were listed. He paused. "I want to show you this so you can back away from pursuing this relationship . . . if you want," he said.

I was taken aback by his openness, yet alarmed his finances were so tight. His budget was stretched to the limit, and he had significant debt. This didn't feel right. I felt he'd exposed this to me a little early in our relationship—too personal, too soon. I didn't know what to say. *Budgets and paychecks are personal matters. Alarm bells began chiming, but I ignored them.*

Our visit lasted another day, and then I drove back home . . . and Christmas.

A week later Ron came to celebrate New Year's Eve and New Year's Day. He'd worked all day, then drove the 250 miles to my home, and he was hungry. "I have something to ask you," he grinned, dropping down onto one knee, "Shirley, will you marry me?" In his hand, he held a small box.

I was astounded. We'd known each other less than two weeks. I liked this guy, sure. He was funny; we seemed to connect in lots of ways. And yes, there was chemistry, too. But marriage? I honestly didn't know what to say. I didn't want to hurt his feelings. In shock, I blurted, "Yes, I will."

There was not the tummy-pinging excitement, relief, or giddiness I'd felt when first Bill and then Blair asked me for my hand in marriage. I honestly felt a little doomed. *What have I gotten myself into? Why did I say yes?* I convinced myself it was okay that the time was so short between our meeting and engagement. It was the same short amount of time as when Blair had asked me. But this felt different. It was dangerous—almost like it wasn't me who said yes but some other person. I'd jumped into a waterfall, hoping I would survive the landing at the bottom.

This story has several red flags to examine. **A red flag is a warning, alerting us that something isn't quite right.**

The first red flag was comparing one man I loved deeply and missed so much with someone new who grew up in the same town. I was very anxious to remarry and have the same beautiful, happy relationship I had with Blair. Surface comparisons won't be accurate in choosing a mate.

The second red flag: Moving too quickly. Ron invited me to come visit his home 250 miles away. We barely knew one another, and he seemed to be rushing things a bit. Just because we connected didn't mean we needed to meet family members so soon. Taking it a bit slower would have been the better route.

The third red flag: Ron showed me his expenses. Too much too soon. Was he warning me in order to provide a way out? We discuss more of this topic in chapter 6.

The fourth red flag: Something was very wrong in his relationship with his wife. Why would she want him out of the house when she was ill? I remembered the precious moments my husband Bill and I had when he was so ill. I wanted to be there with my husband, and he wanted to be with me.

The fifth red flag: Feeling anxious saying yes to his marriage proposal. There should have been excitement, joy, and anticipation of wonderful things to come. I didn't have those feelings.

Why would I ignore those red flags? Because I was anxious to get past my singleness. My marriage to Blair had been so beautiful and I wanted it again. I was lonesome. I thought Ron could fill the void. I was infatuated, not in love. And I was stubborn.

Three Months Later . . .

It was five weeks before our wedding. I was doing my morning meditation—reading my Bible and praying. Without any second thoughts I blurted, "Lord, if this marriage is out of your will, you will need to end it, because I cannot." I was mystified at my words. Later that evening, my phone rang. It was Ron, making his usual evening call to chat.

"Well hi there, you!" I said eagerly.

"Hey."

We talked about our upcoming weekend plans for his daughter and son-in-law and my daughter's family to meet each other at my house. But he seemed strangely subdued, because only a few hours earlier he'd sent me romantic texts about how he missed me.

"What's going on? You seem kind of quiet."

"I've been doing some thinking," he paused. "I don't know if I can say the wedding vows honestly."

"What do you mean? What part of the wedding vows?" My stomach clenched, the tone of my voice raised in defense.

"I don't know if I love you enough," he said flatly. His voice sounded cold and my heart skipped. He continued, "I think we need a break from each other. No talking or texting. I won't come up this weekend."

I was numb from his revelations and didn't know what to say, and the call ended. I went to bed, punched my pillow down, and tried to sleep.

It was over. We didn't get married. I decided to go away for the weekend. I needed some space to pray and think.

My stomach churned as I drove through the winding roads to my destination. With each curve in the road, a beautiful spring scene attempted to capture my attention. I wanted to drive to Ron's home and beg him to change his mind. I longed for his arms around me, yet I was angry at him for breaking it off on the phone instead of face-to-face. I was wounded and wanted to strike out.

As I walked among the early spring gardens, new beginnings of growth showed in the bare, brown palette of the grounds. My heart felt barren too. The early pink cherry blossoms glowed against the dark trunks and reached up to the blue sky, studded with wispy white clouds. I listened to the birds singing, admired the arrogant, yellow daffodils with their large trumpet noses, declaring their joyous sound in color. Yellow and white primroses grew on the ground beneath, preening in the spring sunlight. The friendly faces of the purple and yellow pansies lifted my heart and as I slowly walked back to my room, I knew I would be okay.

I knew the night would be long, and I was prepared for it. I had my Bible nearby. I read,

"I will stand at my watch and station myself on the ramparts; I will look to see what he will say to me" (Habakkuk 2:1 NIV).

I waited. I prayed. I thought back again to the prayer I had said three days earlier: "Oh God, I don't have the strength to do it, but if this marriage is out of your will, then *you* will have to end it."

I asked God for an answer to his perfect will—and he gave it! I also needed to do the work of forgiveness. God was using two imperfect people to do his will in their lives. I begged God to help me move forward. Away from the planned marriage with Ron. Perhaps I would never be married again. I needed to submit my will to God's will. It sounds easy on paper, but not always easy to change the heart. I was doing the work of grief and forgiveness. Sometime soon I knew it would happen. Finally, just before dawn I fell asleep

When I woke later that morning, I was at peace. I was sad. But grateful for the Holy intervention that was so evident in my prayer earlier that week. I knew it was God's best for me—he *had* spoken to me and it was through that prayer, not said by me but by the Holy Spirit, living in me. Though hurt, I knew my heart would heal—if I would allow the Comforter to help with it.

Later that day, I drove home and began adjusting my life back to before Ron. This loss was different than the loss of death. I might have been angry at death itself—but not at God. I knew God would be with me. I wasn't alone.

This story can be a warning to you. We urge you to pay attention if you are making excuses or are rationalizing when you are in the throes of an exciting relationship. Don't be blind to the truth of the person you are with. I've included this story with the hope you can avoid heartache and regret. Stay off this road to nowhere!

Rationalizing and making excuses for someone you want to marry is extremely dangerous. It the most common mistake made in finding a new partner.

Perhaps you've completely grieved your loss—that was death or divorce, but are you really ready to move into a new relationship—a permanent one? If you believe you are in a relationship that is wrong, be proactive and get out of it. Why would you stay in a relationship that is toxic to you? Ending a relationship with too many red flags might be like a sliver you've gotten in your finger that you've tried to ignore. It hurts with the sliver in. It also hurts when taking the sliver out, but the pressure is relieved and it begins to heal—just as you will heal from ending the relationship.

If you believe your partner hasn't grieved their loss, go back to chapter 2 and discuss the key points for moving through grief with them. Ask them relevant questions from the chapter. Be cautious. Remember infatuation does not remove grief and if not fully resolved, the grief will at some point return.

After the "it's over" phone call that spring day, I told God I'd try to be content with being single. I realized I'd made the *idea* of marriage to another partner the *answer* to my loneliness. I was learning I needed to depend on God to fulfill my need for acceptance and love—from One who loves me perfectly. I prayed for resolve, knowing I might never find love like I'd experienced.

I began to enjoy my singleness. I traveled. Hosted dinner parties with my single friends. I was busy speaking, writing, and leading a grief support group. I made dates with myself, which sounds odd, but I knew I needed to learn to enjoy my own company. And I did. When eating out for dinner, I chose a table where I could observe people. I made a game of who the people were and how they lived. I savored my meal and dessert and took time. I attended conferences with a friend. Volunteered at a conference center and made more new friends. Sixteen months passed after the fateful phone call ending my engagement, and I felt I might be ready to meet someone again.

From Jim

"You've got to slow down, Jim!" my pastor said in frustration. "It's only been six months since Kathy died. Don't rush it!"

"I've got it under control, I can make this work, I know I can." I had learned to make things happen in promoting my business, and I thought I needed to do the same with LaRay, the woman I was engaged to. Because the first few years of my marriage to Kathy had been tumultuous, I figured things would work out with LaRay. After all, she was a Christian, the right age, and she was introduced to me by a mutual friend.

Close friends warned me not to move too quick—not fully grieving Kathy's death.

After meeting with my pastor and having honest talks with another close friend, LaRay and I decided we should see a counselor. We were having trouble with our communication. The counselor told me, "Jim, you're like an Italian racehorse—a mover and shaker. LaRay is not. You've overwhelmed her and will continue to do so. I don't think the two of you are going to work."

Soon after our meeting with the counselor, we mutually agreed we weren't right for each other, and we ended our engagement. I was alone again. I felt like I was in love with LaRay, but looking back I realize now it was infatuation.

I wish I could say I'd learned my lesson about moving too quickly, but I hadn't. A few months later, I began dating another woman about my age. Darlene had very different views in important areas of faith, family, and politics. In future chapters, we'll discuss those areas and why they're important.

After several months, I realized Darlene and I would not be compatible even if she would be interested in getting married. Satisfied I'd done the right thing by ending the relationship, I realized I needed to learn to accept my single state.

Purposely I worked hard. I began a home remodel and took the walls down to the bare studs, combined three small bedrooms into two decent-sized ones, and added a bathroom to the master bedroom. I worked hard for hours each day and was pleased with the finished product.

I went on some hiking and camping trips by myself. I begged God to help me be content in whatever circumstances I was in. I asked for his guidance on how to live alone—possibly without a mate for the rest of my life.

We were surprised that engagement breakups are quite common: Statistics say that twenty percent of all engagements are ended. There are many good articles that touch even more on deal breakers and why engagements dissolve.[1] An even stronger statistic comes from Christian authors Jim Burns and Doug Fields in their book that discusses the importance of starting marriages out right. Their statistic is that *one-third* of all engagements dissolve before marriage.[2]

Either statistic reminds us that not all engagements will transition to marriage. That's why paying attention to red flags or deal breakers is important. What if you don't want to give up on the other person? You both believe you do want to get married, despite the red flags? We suggest before you move any further in your relationship that you invest in pre-engagement counseling before you become engaged. The cost of counseling will be worth the investment later on.

You may experience grief if you decide to cut ties with each other. We both can tell you the grief of a broken engagement does not compare to the death of a marriage partner or death of a marriage through divorce. There is loss. There is sometimes embarrassment mixed in with a bit of pride—*why wouldn't he/she want me?* We both experienced shame and betrayal. Yes, your hopes are dashed—for a time. Remember, God wants his best for you in a marriage partner. Don't give up and don't forget the statistics: one-third of engagements do not progress to marriage.

---

[1] https://goo.gl/YBkBkM.
[2] Jim Burns and Doug Fields, *The First Few Years of Marriage: Eight Ways to Strengthen Your "I Do"* (David C. Cook, 2017).

⌒

Are you moving too fast? The questionnaire below will help you determine whether this is possible. Circle your answer to each question. Take it separately, then share and discuss your answers. Give examples or explanations to assist your partner in fully understanding why you answered as you did and provide details that illustrate your point of view.

It is important to compare and discuss your thoughts with each other. Your communication is crucial when considering remarriage. There are no right or wrong answers—just clearly communicated and jointly understood issues that can play a significant role in developing a deep and satisfying marriage. We both agree that in our broken engagements, we would not have even become engaged if we'd read a book like this one.

If you find in answering the first two questions below that there are red flags in your relationship, name them so that you come to a better understanding. If you can't do this with your partner, that's a red flag in itself. It means you don't feel safe enough in the relationship to be honest. That's either an indication that your partner doesn't create an emotionally safe environment for you, or you have personal insecurities in your own heart that need to be healed in order to be a healthy partner in a relationship. At least share these issues with a trusted friend who walks closely with the Lord and who will pray with you.

Questionnaire: Moving Too Fast?

Issues to consider:

1. I think there might be red flags in our relationship.

1	2	3	4	5	6
Strongly Disagree	Disagree	Somewhat Disagree	Somewhat Agree	Agree	Strongly Agree

2. Am I ignoring red flags?

1	2	3	4	5	6
Strongly Disagree	Disagree	Somewhat Disagree	Somewhat Agree	Agree	Strongly Agree

3. Others believe I am ignoring red flags.

1	2	3	4	5	6
Strongly Disagree	Disagree	Somewhat Disagree	Somewhat Agree	Agree	Strongly Agree

4. I am working too hard to make the relationship work.

1	2	3	4	5	6
Strongly Disagree	Disagree	Somewhat Disagree	Somewhat Agree	Agree	Strongly Agree

5. My close friends or family believe I am moving too fast.

1	2	3	4	5	6
Strongly Disagree	Disagree	Somewhat Disagree	Somewhat Agree	Agree	Strongly Agree

6. My close friends and family are afraid this relationship will break my heart.

1	2	3	4	5	6
Strongly Disagree	Disagree	Somewhat Disagree	Somewhat Agree	Agree	Strongly Agree

Suggested Discussion Guide for your answers

Some suggested ways you and/or your potential mate might want to take a closer look when discussing your answers:

First, if you score a lot of 3's and 4's this might indicate a number of vaguely veiled potential disagreements because there was neither strongly agreed or disagreed statements of your preferences. Make sure you have fully discussed and analyzed any large gaps on a particular question such as one person rating a statement with a 1, 2, or 3, and the other person rating the same question 4, 5, or 6. These could be potential "red flags" and down the road could also be "deal breakers."

Second, if both of you are filling out the questionnaire, do this separately and then discuss your concerns with your potential partner. From your answers to the questionnaire, list what you feel could be the red flags (be honest!) to this potential relationship. Before you share these with your partner, you may want to list potential red flags with a good friend to make sure your answers are as honest as they can be. Be cautious; you might be filled with romantic feelings and/or infatuation, and your answers may be biased or prevent you from honestly identifying potential red flags.

Third, you can also discuss areas of agreement, which will assist in deepening your relationship.

When people are courting or starting a long-term relationship, they are acting out of their most gracious, flexible, and accommodating mindsets and mannerisms. Small issues now have the likelihood of becoming big issues after the honeymoon period is over. We encourage you to pay attention to red flags. Listen to close friends and their reaction to the relationship you're involved in. Talk to God and listen to the Holy Spirit within you. Be honest with yourself if you sense you have reservations.

We've stressed the importance of red flags and moving too fast. There's another area you should seriously consider: do you share the same faith?

Don't forget to listen to the song to set the scene for the next chapter!

Chapter Five ✐

Faith

♪ "You Raise Me Up" ♪
Brendan Graham

*I*t had been a long five days. My husband Bill had been hospitalized nearly a week and we still had no answers. The side effects of the meds one doctor had prescribed for the post-herpetic pain Bill had were scary. For unknown reasons, while walking, Bill would collapse to the floor without warning. We wanted pain relief without these side effects.

On Saturday morning, the female hospital chaplain prayed with us and read Scripture. I wept as she read and prayed. "Our Father, please help Bill and Shirley as they cope with this illness. Be their strength and song during this difficult time."

Late that Saturday night I sat by my husband's bedside while he slept. I felt the darkness of the room closing in around me as despair clenched my heart. Then, note by note, I caught the sounds of singing. *Precious Lord, Take My hand/Lead me on, let me stand/I am tired, I am weak, I am worn*

The rich alto voice continued to lift old hymns. I stood, amazed, and followed the melody down the hall. A few doors down, I glanced into a darkened room and saw a black woman, wearing a black and white dress, sitting in a bedside chair. She would never know the comfort she gave a neighbor that evening. I tiptoed back to Bill's room, knowing I was not alone . . .

Next morning, I ventured to the room where I'd heard the singing and found it empty. The bed was made and no one was there. I'm not sure if the patient had died, or had it been a visit by an angel to comfort me? It was a moment I won't forget that helped me through the next months and years, reminding me I was not alone.

Our relationship with Jesus—a vertical relationship with God—is the most important relationship we can enjoy. It is eternal, and while a wonderful gift from God, marriage is only temporary. Keep that in mind as you develop your relationship.

When you choose to marry, it is important to share your faith story. Faith in Jesus Christ is important for both parties in a marriage. You may think you can marry someone you love who does not believe. The Bible is quite clear about becoming partners with someone who is not a believer: "Do not become partners with those who do not believe, for what partnership is there between righteousness and lawlessness, or what fellowship does light have with darkness?" (2 Corinthians 7:14 NET).

We are both acquainted with Christians who are married to unbelievers. Though some may have satisfying marriages, we also know of those where sharp discord eventually led to divorce. Faith is an important aspect of life that influences church attendance, preferences for movie watching, even end-of-life directives. Why would you want to share one of the most important aspects of your life with someone who doesn't share your beliefs? Take caution here.

When we both were widowed—Shirley in 2006 and 2010; Jim in 2011—we both knew if we married again, we'd want a spouse to be a rock-solid follower of Jesus Christ. We knew it would also be helpful if their church denomination was similar. When we joined an online matching service, we both wanted to be sure our profiles clearly indicated our religious beliefs and denominational preference. At our first meeting, we shared our faith stories as well as our stories of loss. Both were important. And we were delighted we shared similar beliefs.

From Jim

I was raised in a very religious home where we attended Mass regularly. I was an altar boy, had my first communion, and attended parochial school for twelve years where I received a good education and learned Catholic traditions.

Sister Mary Theresa, my sixth-grade teacher, asked, "Would anyone like to volunteer for a prayer vigil next week?" She reminded us this was serious business and yes, we'd get out of class. "This is not a time to fool around, but pray," she warned. I was one of the first to sign up, excited to volunteer. Sure, I got out of class, but I really wanted to do the prayer vigil. I always enjoyed going into the church by myself. There were flickering candles, with the smell of incense in the air. It was peaceful and quiet. I enjoyed the mystery, and that day I did pray during my allotted time. The dim and quiet places are still my favorite way to retreat, to think, pray, and read.

During my first marriage to Margi, we were nominal Catholics and attended Mass most Sundays. Yet I was troubled by some of the people I knew attending Mass. They seemed pious during Mass and at confession; but in conversation, I saw them yelling at their families or bragging how they avoided paying taxes they owed. I pondered, *Are all churchgoers like this?* I hoped it wasn't true, but it disturbed me.

Because of the pressures of raising three kids, launching my career and traveling a lot, and Margi working full time as an RN at Good Samaritan Hospital, we began to drift apart.

Soon, we were living more like roommates who shared the same bed. We tried different things to improve our situation. We attended Marriage Encounter, a weekend marriage retreat that helped us for a short time, but soon we reverted back to our old roles: roommates raising three kids.

In the late seventies, the church I attended did not provide help for floundering marriages.

In seeking answers to find help for our troubled marriage, we enrolled in a personal development program called Erhard Seminar and Training (EST). Little did I know that the concepts of EST would finish our marriage.

The core beliefs of EST state that we are the cause of all reality and are the gods of our reality. It made sense to me at the time, but as I now describe their core beliefs, I realize how wrong the whole concept was.

EST encouraged us to find other seekers to attend the intensive weekend that used a variety of brain-washing activities. The two weekends would consist of eighteen-hour days of emotionally draining, mind-altering training exercises. The leadership used group pressure on the participants to conform.

In EST, we were encouraged to be free agents in our relationships, leading to unfaithfulness in some marriages—including ours. The training encouraged couples to read the book *Open Marriage*. Our marriage was ripped apart, and we were never able to reconcile. Within the year, we were separated; we divorced a year later.

After my divorce, I was apart from my children on a daily basis. I made two commitments—and kept them—after the divorce: Always pay the monthly support for the children on time. Never say anything negative about their mother in front of them. The court allowed me visitation every Thursday and every other weekend. I was devastated. Broken. Betrayed. EST hadn't helped. Even regular church attendance didn't help. I continued to attend weekly Mass, but I missed my children desperately. I began questioning the value of going to church at all. I believed there was a God, but I didn't see any relevance to my broken situation. I continued to seek the truth, and during those times of doubt, I had a conversation with a woman named Kathy. She challenged me to examine the claims of Jesus Christ. That he was a real person who claimed to be God's son. He loved humans so much that he died for their sins—and the best part of all—was resurrected from the dead.

I believed all of that in my head—they taught those things in parochial school and church—but I didn't believe it in my heart. I began to realize Jesus was more than a statue that I gazed at every Sunday at Mass. He was a real person.

Kathy suggested I read some books that she found helpful in discovering truths in the Bible. Those books, *Evidence that Demands a Verdict* and *More than a Carpenter*, convinced and convicted me that the Bible was really true. There was a God who died for the sins of the world, including mine, and then was resurrected from the dead. I studied the books, read evidence in the Bible, and pored over the questions at the end of the books. When I came to the conclusion those things were true, I realized I needed to repent of my selfish attitudes, my broken marriage, and most of all, my desire to control every aspect of my life. One evening, it all made sense. I asked Jesus to forgive me of my sins—the ones he died for—and take control of my heart and life.

Instead of just going to Mass Sunday mornings or Saturday evenings, I began devouring the Bible. Jesus began to be my guide. Not only was he my Savior, he was also my friend. He comforted me like no one else could. The pain and rejection of the divorce and the lost time with my kids was almost more than I could take.

But Jesus was always there. I could talk to him anytime. He understood. He loved me and accepted me just the way I was. Gradually, I began to change, wanting to please God and respond to people in a godly way.

Jesus was once asked by a Torah scholar what the most important commandment was and he answered, *Love the Lord your God with all your heart and with all your soul and with all your mind and with all your strength. The second is this: Love your neighbor as yourself* (Mark 12:29–31 NIV).

Those words resonated with me. I joined an evangelical church that taught the Bible in a practical and relevant way that I didn't experience in the Catholic church. Within a year, I was baptized to demonstrate my personal commitment to Christ.

My life has never been the same since I took that step more than thirty years ago.

Nearly two years later, I married Kathy . . .

There have been really hard times since then. My stepdaughter, Kara, whom I helped raise, died suddenly of sleep apnea at age thirty-one. It was devastating—I loved her as my own daughter. Yet God was there, comforting Kathy and me as we struggled with our grief.

About a year later, we found out Kathy had a terminal illness that couldn't be helped by treatment. Three years after the diagnosis, Kathy died. I reeled with the loss. But again, he was there.

From Shirley

Like Jim, I always had a heart toward God. I wanted to know all about the Bible and loved going to Sunday School and Vacation Bible School. At a young age, I seemed to understand many of the truths in the Bible, and one afternoon I prayed a simple prayer—telling him I was sorry for things I'd done wrong. I asked him to forgive me and come into my heart. I told him I wanted to go to heaven when I died. In my childlike faith, I believed and understood. I knew I was a sinner, that I did things my own way—which is actually what sin is: wanting to do things on my time and my own way.

My life became forever linked with Jesus. After saying that prayer, my decisions were different.

There were times when I didn't read the Bible and sometimes I did things the way I wanted to instead of considering what God would want me to do. At a pivotal moment in my adult life—when my daughter, Erika, was born and nearly died—God got my attention. Since that commitment forty-five years ago, he has been my rock and guide. I want to live a life pleasing to him and share that story with others.

God was very near to me during the early rocky years of my first marriage. He was close to me when the doctor told me at thirty-four weeks into my pregnancy my baby was dead. I have already written how difficult and devastating losing two spouses was. I can't imagine myself going through such difficulty without Jesus, the best Comforter anyone could have.

What if one of you is not as spiritually mature as the other? If they are willing to develop their Christian faith, it gives opportunity for both of you to grow. When Jim and Kathy married, she was the stronger Christian, but Jim wanted to learn more. As a result, his faith grew and together they served in their church and community.

For us, from our first "hello" we experienced an instant spiritual connection. We prayed together at our first meeting. Our second date included attending a worship service together. We experienced a spiritual intimacy because of our mutual beliefs. The spiritual intimacy is just as important as physical intimacy.

~

The questionnaire below will help you identify potential challenges to your union in the area of faith. Circle your answer to each question. Take it separately, then share and discuss your answers. Give examples or explanations to assist your partner in fully understanding why you answered as you did and provide details that illustrate your point of view.

Remember, communication is crucial when considering remarriage. There are no right or wrong answers—just clearly communicated and jointly understood issues that can play a significant role in developing a deep and satisfying marriage.

Questionnaire: Faith

Issues to consider:

1. We share the same background in our belief in God.

1	2	3	4	5	6
Strongly Disagree	Disagree	Somewhat Disagree	Somewhat Agree	Agree	Strongly Agree

2. I am comfortable in a traditional worship setting.

1	2	3	4	5	6
Strongly Disagree	Disagree	Somewhat Disagree	Somewhat Agree	Agree	Strongly Agree

3. I am comfortable in a charismatic/Pentecostal style of worship.

1	2	3	4	5	6
Strongly Disagree	Disagree	Somewhat Disagree	Somewhat Agree	Agree	Strongly Agree

4. We share the same Christian worship styles.

1	2	3	4	5	6
Strongly Disagree	Disagree	Somewhat Disagree	Somewhat Agree	Agree	Strongly Agree

5. I bring religious/biblical values into my daily decision making.

1	2	3	4	5	6
Strongly Disagree	Disagree	Somewhat Disagree	Somewhat Agree	Agree	Strongly Agree

6. Jesus Christ is an important aspect in my daily life.

1	2	3	4	5	6
Strongly Disagree	Disagree	Somewhat Disagree	Somewhat Agree	Agree	Strongly Agree

7. I wish to attend church on a regular basis.

1	2	3	4	5	6
Strongly Disagree	Disagree	Somewhat Disagree	Somewhat Agree	Agree	Strongly Agree

8. I am open to changing where I attend church to worship with my future spouse.

1	2	3	4	5	6
Strongly Disagree	Disagree	Somewhat Disagree	Somewhat Agree	Agree	Strongly Agree

There are additional discussion ideas found in the appendix.

Jointly sharing your journey of faith is an important element in a relationship. Take the time to hear how God has worked throughout each of your lives.

Next, we'll discuss financial affairs. We found seeking an attorney was helpful. How about you? We recommend you don't neglect this important step.

Don't forget to listen to the next song that will set the stage!

Chapter Six ∽

What's Mine is Yours?

♪ "Can't Buy Me Love" ♪
The Beatles

"*They* won't let me have anything," Betty sobbed. "I can't even get into the house. I wish we'd seen an attorney!" she exclaimed. She'd been happily married for the second time to Frank, but they hadn't bothered to have a will or a prenuptial agreement drawn up. Shortly after their marriage, Frank had medical tests revealing he had cancer, and he died within the first year of their marriage. Everything reverted to his children legally. His children didn't allow her to go back into their residence even to retrieve her own personal belongings.

The story above is a good example of why a couple—Christian or not—should have a prenup drawn up. No couple plans to divorce as they say their vows, but death is guaranteed in the future for either person. The prenup is to protect each person's assets and inheritance for their children and designated charities. This should be your decision, not the state's, nor the widow/widower, nor children of the second marriage.

From Shirley

Before my second marriage, Blair and I each contacted our own attorney and had a prenuptial (prenup) agreement written and signed. We married, and though we'd met with our joint attorney to draw up our last will and testament, we didn't sign the last will and testament. When Blair died suddenly, the prenup was the legal document to finish his estate. I was glad we had drawn it up.

When Jim and I were engaged, I went to a family law attorney and had a prenuptial agreement drawn up again. Both parties needed to sign each agreement, and when it was time to sign the final papers, Jim came with me and signed where he needed to. After compiling our financial records, divorce or death certificates, beneficiary names and their personal data, *and* paying quite a sum of money, we left.

In spite of the energy and money spent in drawing up the agreement, we had a sense of release.

Six happy months passed as Mr. and Mrs. Mozena. One of Jim's dreams was to purchase a motor home and drive around the United States. Motor homes are costly, and though we would be able to purchase one, we weren't sure how to combine our money to do it. I wanted reassurances we could afford both an RV and our home. Fearful thoughts of sudden death crossed my mind—even though I knew God would take care of me as he had in the past. I wondered, *What if Jim dies? Will I be financially able to stay in our home? Will the RV belong to me?*

"Honey," Jim said, "I think it's time to see our attorney about our last will and testament. I don't know how the laws in Washington State compare to Oregon's. There's my money, your money, and what we want to leave our kids and grandkids. I think an attorney might help us sort it out. Let's make an appointment with the attorney you used with Blair."

"I agree. I always regretted Bill and I didn't have our wills drawn up . . . I don't want to be in limbo now about our finances."

We knew a will needed to be written. I remember with heartbreak my time with Blair was unexpectedly shorter than we ever believed—but the legal aspects were taken care of.

It was expensive and more complicated with previous marriages and stepchildren involved. His kids. My kids. Stepkids on both sides. There are previous wishes from our late spouses. There are special instructions for expenses, and we have "our" account. Shirley's account. Jim's account. It's clearly stated.

When we married, we each sold our residences and purchased a home together. The state of Washington, where we live, is a community property state.

> "Community property" is everything a husband and wife own together. This typically includes all money earned, debts incurred, and property acquired during the marriage. Community property states classify the following as a married couple's joint property:
>
> 1. Any income received by either spouse during the marriage.
> 2. Any real or personal property acquired with income earned during the marriage. This includes, vehicles, homes, furniture, appliances, and luxury items.
> 3. Any debts acquired during the marriage.[3]

[3] Christine Fletcher, "10 Things You Need to Know About Prenups," *Forbes Magazine*, September 18, 2018.

A prenuptial agreement is a private agreement between a couple signed before they get married that sets forth the division of their assets in the event of divorce or death. Each state has its own laws regarding the enforcement and validity of prenuptial agreements.

Which state's law to apply depends on where the marriage took place, where the parties live during the marriage, and what law the agreement says to apply.

The laws vary within each state, so we suggest when you are engaged, make an appointment with a family attorney, bring all your paperwork, and let the professionals help you. Sitting in an attorney's office, discussing end-of-life details is not pleasant, but it is necessary. What if you cannot afford a prenup? There are some free online downloads. There are also legal sites to put together your wills. Obviously, you know your financial situation better than anyone else, but we believe getting professional help—either on the internet or with a local attorney is the best option.

We are glad we took the step of retaining an attorney and having a prenup prepared. There was a sense of relief when our will was drawn up and signed. There won't be any disputes when our days are ended.

The questionnaire below will help you identify potential challenges to your union in the area of finances and assets. Circle your answer to each question as honestly as you can. Take it separately, then share and discuss your answers. Give examples or explanations to assist your partner in fully understanding why you answered as you did and provide details that illustrate your point of view.

Remember, communication is crucial when considering re-marriage. There are no right or wrong answers—just clearly communicated and jointly understood issues that can play a significant role in developing a deep and satisfying marriage.

Questionnaire: What's Mine is Yours?

Issues to consider:

1. I believe in blending all our financial resources.

1	2	3	4	5	6
Strongly Disagree	Disagree	Somewhat Disagree	Somewhat Agree	Agree	Strongly Agree

2. I have shared with my potential mate all my savings and debt(s) I currently have.

1	2	3	4	5	6
Strongly Disagree	Disagree	Somewhat Disagree	Somewhat Agree	Agree	Strongly Agree

3. I believe a prenuptial agreement might be helpful in describing our individual desires relating how our financial resources will be shared upon our death and/or termination of relationship.

1	2	3	4	5	6
Strongly Disagree	Disagree	Somewhat Disagree	Somewhat Agree	Agree	Strongly Agree

4. I am willing to sign a prenuptial agreement.

1	2	3	4	5	6
Strongly Disagree	Disagree	Somewhat Disagree	Somewhat Agree	Agree	Strongly Agree

5. I have a "Will and Trust" and believe it would be helpful to draw one up for our relationship.

1	2	3	4	5	6
Strongly Disagree	Disagree	Somewhat Disagree	Somewhat Agree	Agree	Strongly Agree

6. I have a clear idea how we should share our daily and monthly expenses.

1	2	3	4	5	6
Strongly Disagree	Disagree	Somewhat Disagree	Somewhat Agree	Agree	Strongly Agree

7. I have shared my financial plans for retirement.

1	2	3	4	5	6
Strongly Disagree	Disagree	Somewhat Disagree	Somewhat Agree	Agree	Strongly Agree

8. I have a clear understanding of what our housing arrangements would be (i.e., joint purchase of home, live in current home, etc.).

1	2	3	4	5	6
Strongly Disagree	Disagree	Somewhat Disagree	Somewhat Agree	Agree	Strongly Agree

There are additional discussion ideas found in the appendix.

Discussing money and legal issues is always difficult, but you've taken a big step in taking the questionnaire and talking about it. Our next chapter will be challenging as well, but we believe worthy of consideration. Blending families can be tricky. Don't forget to listen to the chapter theme song!

Chapter Seven ⟳

Yours, Mine, Ours! Blending Families

♪ "We Are Family" ♪
Nile Rodgers/Bernard Edwards

Marrying again involves blending families. No matter that the children are raised and out of the home. There's still my kids and his kids. My grands and his grands. It really doesn't matter if this is a second or third marriage. Every marriage is a blended family even the first time.

We both came from long-term marriages, and there was a lot of history in them.

From Jim

When I pledged wedding vows to Margi, I meant them. It's true, we were practically kids on that March day in 1969. I was not even twenty years old. After ten years of marriage, Margi and I separated. I moved into an apartment near our family home and zeroed in on my job. Our divorce was finalized a year or so later. The court awarded Margi full custody of the children, with visitation each Thursday evening and every other weekend for me. Those every-other weekends and Thursday evenings were always on my calendar, and I never scheduled anything during that time. But that wasn't what I wanted; it just wasn't enough. I loved my kids and wanted to be with them all the time. I hated it that they didn't live with me every day. I was a broken-hearted, part-time dad.

My heart ached like a sore tooth because I was separated from my kids. I've always been a take-charge type of guy, though anxiety hummed at a low ebb in my brain constantly. But during and after the divorce, the anxiety morphed into a nearly always-present roar of overwhelming dread that threatened to drown me and my family like a tidal wave.

I love my three kids, and I had never dreamed I'd be a divorced father. Vicki, my oldest daughter, was twelve at the time of the final decree and fiercely loyal to her mother. Mostly, she chose not to spend those awarded times with me. I wanted to believe she was torn between loving both her parents yet wanting to be loyal to her mother. It was different with the boys. Kevin was nine, and Bryan, seven. They seemed eager to spend weekends and Thursday evenings with me.

While I was a divorced, single dad, I worked for Kaiser Permanente. A coworker suggested I meet her friend. My life was crazy. My job was stressful, my kids no longer lived with me. It was enough just getting through my days and trying to be with my kids as much as possible and I resisted meeting her for several months, but one lonely night I relented and gave her a call. Her name was Kathy Epperson.

Kathy was a tall, blonde, attractive woman, and a business manager for Kaiser Permanente. What became more important than her looks and business savvy, however, was her strong Christian faith.

On our dates, we had earnest conversations about our pasts and the mistakes we'd both made in our previous marriages. She was the one who pointed me to a personal relationship with Jesus Christ, one like she had.

Kathy and I continued to date and within several months, I asked her to marry me. "I'd like to think about it." After a week, she said, "Yes."

Our wedding took place in a large home with a spectacular view above the Columbia River Gorge. We invited a few close friends and family to witness the event that beautiful October evening. My daughter, Vicki (now fourteen), was a junior bridesmaid, and my sons Kevin (now ten) and Bryan (now eight) were junior grooms-men. Kathy's son, Ryan (now thirteen), was also a groomsman, and her daughter, Kara (seven), the flower girl.

I wish I could say having begun my personal relationship with Christ and having met and married a Christ-follower that all was perfect afterward. But it was not.

The first morning after our honeymoon in that swanky hotel in Victoria, we gazed at the colorful autumn orange and gold trees just outside our window, sipped our coffee, and dug into our Eggs Benedict. We strategized our schedule for our return home later that week.

Real life began to morph into view and the newness and excite-ment of the wedding faded as we both realized that day, life would be a lot more complicated than the idyllic honeymoon we were experiencing.

We both pushed aside the heavy thoughts because we *were* married and resolved to make the best of a complicated future. Blending our two families, values, and traditions maybe wouldn't be as easy as we envisioned.

My stepchildren Ryan and Kara lived with us full time, and my sons Kevin and Bryan, and sometimes Vicki, were with us every other weekend and every Thursday evening. I was now a part-time dad and a full-time stepfather.

Our marriage was a little like water running over the spillway of a dam: forceful and swift. Kathy came from a dysfunctional marriage and so did I. Our children were the flotsam and jetsam of those marriages. Betrayals, financial challenges of supporting two families, and different methods of child raising were the debris. From both sides. It wasn't easy for any of us: not for Kathy, not for my ex-wife Margi, and not for me. But these issues and more were especially difficult for the children—and eventually, the grandchildren. *They* didn't choose this, nor would they have.

I tried to squeeze everything into weekends with my kids. Late Sunday afternoon came all too quickly, and driving my children home I'd say, "Did you remember to pack all of your homework in your backpack? Don't forget, I'll pick you up this Thursday. We'll have a great time." I tried to be as positive and cheerful as I could, "I'll pick you up on Thursday, right after school, okay?"

"Okay," they'd chime as they scooted out of the car, their attention already focused on entering their other life—the one where they lived with a stepdad and their mother.

I rubbed the tears away with my fist as I drove home, the reality of everyone's loss because of the divorce. *Why did this happen to me? I never wanted this and here I am, driving home to Kathy and her kids and leaving my own behind.*

As I drove up the long, narrow driveway to the old farmhouse, I readjusted to my other life—the one with my wife Kathy and her two children, where I was the stepdad to Kara and Ryan.

My stepchildren's father, Ray, lived in another state and was only available a few times a year. He was a "Disneyland Dad"—the dad who could buy treats and clothing, take them to exciting places. Me, well, I was there on a daily basis. But I wasn't their father; I often felt like I wasn't their dad either. They called me Jim and sometimes would remind me I wasn't their dad. It's true, I wasn't their bio-dad. Ray was. But on a day-to-day basis, that's what I was being: their dad.

"You're not my dad!" My stepdaughter, Kara, flung the words

at me like a slap in the face. I'd just told her to clean up her room one day when her mom was at work. She didn't want to do the task and told me so. The phrase: *When the dad's not the father, and the father's not the dad* fit me to a "T."

Two years after we were married, Ryan announced he wanted to live with his dad. It broke Kathy's heart to release him to his father, who lived in faraway California, but she felt she had no choice.

We stumbled through as those difficult months turned into years. We argued about raising a strong-willed child. Kathy said I favored my kids and was harder on hers. She claimed I didn't love them as I did my own. She was probably right.

One Sunday afternoon, we were driving in the Columbia River Gorge, enjoying the beautiful fall foliage being displayed on the hills nearby. We stopped off at Crown Point, where millions visit each year. We laughed at the sign that read "Vista House will be closed when the winds are 50 MPH or more."

That beautiful day was a riot of orange, red, and yellow against the dark green of the evergreens along the steep ridges of the gorge. We fell in love with the area. As we drove, we turned toward Corbett, a small community nestled in the middle of the gorge. We gazed at the beautiful farms and hills studded with trees and giant rocks. As we wound around one road we had impulsively turned onto, we saw a "for sale" sign. "Let's see what this is," Kathy said.

"It says 'appointment only.' We don't have an appointment; do you think it will be okay to drive onto their property?"

"Oh, let's just do it. It's so pretty here."

We wound up the steep, curved driveway and pulled up to a farmhouse that looked like it had been built in the early part of the century. Of the five-acre parcel, one-half acre was dedicated to a variety of beautiful dahlias that were proudly completing their bloom season. A worn sign near the top of the driveway said, *Lost Acres Dahlia Farm.* Vine maples were turning a burgundy color that contrasted with the dark-green Douglas firs. A ramshackle barn stood on one edge of the property.

An elderly man and his wife were sitting in the warm autumn sun on the porch. They greeted us as we got out of the car. He startled us with his greeting. "Hello Jim and Kathy. Are you the people who want to buy our house? We've been praying for ya!" he joked.

We didn't understand. How did he know our names? After a few minutes, he explained they sat right behind us regularly at the church we all attended. We were surprised, but also felt like our meeting at this time was all part of God's plan for us. Before we left that afternoon, we'd agreed with them we wanted to purchase their property.

The house needed a lot of work as did the surrounding five acres, but we loved the view of the Sandy River Gorge just below us. It was quiet and beautiful.

The bright orange shag carpeting was matted down in places, the kitchen cupboards were worn and would need to be replaced, but we loved it. Soon we were the owners of the place we renamed *Lost Acres*.

We began planning what to do first to make it a livable place for us. It would be a stretch for our budget because the house would not be ready for us to move in for several months. That meant we would be making two mortgage payments. We also wanted to wait until school was out for my stepdaughter, Kara, who was in middle school. Some people wondered why we'd give up a nice home on a golf course, but we were determined this was the place for us.

It turned out to be the best thing for our marriage, and we enjoyed that piece of heaven for twenty-five years. We learned, however, that the weather was not the picture perfect one we enjoyed that first day we saw the place. There's a lot of wind and ice storms there, and the following winter was a cold, icy, snowy one. But it was all good. We'd found our home and we were happy.

We found a small community church nearby, became members, and began to make lifelong friends. Kara joined the youth group, made friends, and liked the smaller classes in the nearby Corbett School.

We both agreed it was the purchase of that piece of property and landscaping the acreage and remodeling the house that gave a new focus to our marriage. Looking back, I believe it saved our marriage at a time when it was near crisis mode.

We were active in the church and community. Kathy worked full time and I'd now begun a fledgling consulting business in the health care and energy industries.

Our children grew. My daughter, Vicki, married first, and later Kevin and Bryan. Then Kathy's kids, Ryan and Kara, married also. Soon they began having children. Between us we had nine grandchildren. At first we tried to have Mozena/Epperson family events together at major holidays, but eventually, it became too complicated. Trying to be at three places in one day—or even the next, became too hard for the young grandchildren. Kathy and I decided to eliminate the major Christmas/Thanksgiving dinners and invited the grands over separately. We had cookie baking together with all of the grandchildren and then went for a "Polar Express" train ride or visited the zoo and rode the "Zoolights Train." Then we gave them their presents. Our Christmases with the two of us were quiet events. It's true you need to adapt when the family is blended.

From Shirley

There were flaws in my first marriage of forty years. After stumbling along with dysfunction for more than half of those years, we finally found a way to communicate, which made a world of difference. We learned to repeat things back to each other, really listening to what the other was saying instead of just wanting to be heard ourselves. It seems such a simple thing, yet we had to let go of our stubbornness in thinking the other person needed to change. That key element made a major change in our marriage.

Because of the difficulties in my first marriage to Bill, I felt better equipped to address any problems that came in blending a family. It helped that my children, Todd and Erika, were grown. Blair's sons, Greg and Jonathan, were adults too. It seemed our families blended especially well. My youngest four grandchildren addressed Blair as Grandpa Blair and he lovingly called them "the tribe." It's sad to me that he never met his own biological grandchildren, for they were born after he died. I know he'd be glad that I've attempted to keep up with them now.

Both Greg and Jonathan were very happy for their dad in marrying me. They saw how lonely he was without their mother, Patricia. They even had their special names for me: Ma and Mama Shirley. I was thrilled to have two more kids to add to my brood. There were travels to Colorado at Christmastime to meet Greg's in-laws who wintered there. Greg and his wife, Caytie, were there. Jonathan came, too. We ate, played games, and laughed. Blair, with the other guys, watched multiple Bowl games on New Year's Day.

I met Blair's in-laws when we traveled to South Africa. They were thrilled for Blair that he was married and happy again . . . and then suddenly, Blair was gone.

After he died, Blair's sons supported me emotionally and completely accepted their father's wishes after he died. "We want to honor what Dad wanted," they both said as we sat in the attorney's office and reviewed the legal papers. In the prenuptial, I was given a life estate, which meant I was free to live in the residence that was in Blair's name and where we lived when we married. I made changes to the home we shared. I repainted our bedroom that was now my bedroom, added new photos, and found a new print in red and black I added to the walls.

Blair's two sons, Greg and Jonathan, continued to keep in touch. I traveled to Pittsburgh to meet Greg and Caytie's firstborn daughter and later visited them in Germany while Greg was on a writing sabbatical.

Jonathan and I met in San Francisco where he now lived.

It was the first anniversary of Blair's death. I had to go somewhere, be with someone who understood. I flew to the city to stay with my brother and his wife, and at the same time, to visit Jonathan to celebrate his birthday. We played dominoes, ate birthday cake, and wonderful food my sister-in-law, Lexie, prepared. Sunday morning as we walked through the farmer's market and I was feeling sad, Jonathan came up to me and put his arm around me, asking, "You doing' okay, boss?"

"No, I'm not."

That was all the conversation. We both understood we'd have these moments for some time to come. We mourned together.

Four years later . . .

To my surprise and joy, both stepsons flew in from out of town for my wedding ceremony to Jim. Greg was part of the ceremony in giving the blessing prayer.

After our honeymoon, we finished cleaning out the house Blair and I shared, getting it ready for the boys to sell. Texts and emails flew back and forth with questions about what to do with certain items. Blair had carefully planned which furnishings and housewares he wanted to remain in the family and they were packed and given to the boys. Yet there was still a mountain of things to move out of the house, and I was responsible to disperse the duplicate items we didn't need. Many items that weren't specified I kept, or they went to charity. It took about a month to clear everything out of the house and it was ready to be put on the market.

I was frustrated when Jonathan continued to question where certain items were. I felt like he was overreacting. *Please pack up our personal Christmas decorations and send them to my address* he texted one day. He asked about minuscule items I didn't think he would even care about. Perhaps it was his way of grieving the final loss of both of his parents.

We do communicate somewhat regularly with Greg and have

visited them numerous times at their home in Iowa. We consider his four daughters our grandchildren, though of course there is no blood relation. We try to keep up with them though they live five states away from us. I made a promise to Blair I would be "grammie" to his children and do the best I could though they live 2,000 miles away.

Our Blended Family

Blending families can be difficult. When the children are out of the home, it makes it less complicated, but it still is not easy. Between the two of us, we now have eight children. Shirley came into the marriage with a son, Todd, and daughter, Erika, and two stepsons, Greg, who lives in Iowa, and Jonathan, who lives in California.

Jim has a daughter, Vicki, and two sons, Kevin and Bryan. His stepson Ryan lives in California. Jim's stepdaughter Kara is deceased and survived by his stepson-in-law, Aaron, who lives nearby. That makes eight.

Our combined grands (step and biological) number twenty. They are blessings and we're glad we have them, but it is not necessarily easy. Our home is quite spacious, but if all the kids and grands were to come at the same time, we wouldn't have room. Instead, we've opted to invite the families in smaller units, such as Jim's kids and grands, my kids and grands. That means more preparation time but that's okay. We enjoy entertaining and interacting with our extended families. Our schedules can be hectic because we want to be involved as much as we can with special events in our loved one's lives.

Some of the grands address us by our first names—which is fine with us. Jim's grands call him Grandpa, some of my grands call him Grandpa Jim. Some of the stepgrands call me Grammie. We want them to feel comfortable with whatever they call us.

It can be true that some adult children really aren't interested in continuing a relationship with a stepmom or stepdad. We've experienced polite "no thank-yous" more often than not, though we do our best to stay connected. Sometimes life doesn't turn out the way we want it to.

Jim has a positive attitude when it comes to his children. There have been disappointments throughout his adult life-after-divorce. He has learned to let it go and be grateful for whatever time he does have with each of his kids. Jim learned that being positive is the best way to cope with a situation that could be filled with resentments that don't help kids or grandkids.

For example, we invite all the family to special events such as a birthday celebration, Christmas, or other holidays. One family member doesn't respond at all. I get upset, "Why doesn't so-and-so bother to answer our invitation?"

Jim responds with a "But aren't you glad the other two want to come?" He is grateful for the ones who say they'll be there. Instead of being disappointed or upset when an invitation is turned down, he will look on the bright side that some have said yes. I've learned a lot about positivity from Jim in blending a family. It *is* complicated, but possible!

In the fall and spring, two of our grandsons are in track. Two granddaughters swim. There's end-of-the year awards assemblies, weddings, showers, birthdays—all the myriad of activities in a family. Totally normal. It's just we have a lot of them!

If you both are on board with including all your children and grandchildren in your day-to-day activities, go for it, but know your schedule will be full and you won't be able to fit all of them in. We do our best but are not always successful. At some point, we realize the grands will be grown and busy in their own lives, so we want to make the most of these active days. Make the most of your blended family situation and be grateful you have them in your life.

We spent a June Friday in the bright sun, watching Caleb—grandson on Shirley's side—participate in the US Junior Olympics. He finished third place in the decathlon and went on to regionals. We weren't able to go because we had a family wedding to attend—Jim's oldest granddaughter, Taylor. She was married outdoors in the late afternoon above the Willamette River. We squeezed hands as they said their vows to each other, reminding us of the vows we'd pledged to each other nearly five years ago.

There were toasts, a first dance for the bride and groom, as well as father/daughter, mother/son dances. It was a happy event with just a teensy bit of awkwardness. This part of the family is also part of the brokenness of his first marriage. Jim's former wife and grandmother of the bride, Margi, was there with politeness all around. But I felt a whisper of sadness for Jim. We didn't sit at the table with his children, I assume because they thought it would be awkward with the two divorced parents at the same table. I really think it would have been fine. All bumpy parts of wrong choices made decades ago. Instead, we sat at a different table with Jim's siblings.

More recently, we completed a cruise with part of the family. In many ways, we anticipated the event with a bit of dread. Would everyone get along? Would they be aloof? It turned out to be a wonderful event. Family members got to know each other better and we shared experiences and outings together. Although the entire family was not able to attend, both sides were represented. It was good.

There are less expensive things than a cruise you can do with your blended family. We're finding it isn't possible to include everyone all the time. It's better to interact with one or two families at a time. We enjoy taking the older grands to lunch for their birthdays as a good way to connect with them on a one-to-one basis.

At Christmas time, we prepare dinner for the extended family, but not necessarily on December 25. This year, we have set aside a day before Christmas with Shirley's kids. We will have a day with some of Jim's kids and grandkids another Saturday after Christmas. We invite whoever can come on Christmas or Thanksgiving, with openness. We understand that as families grow it makes it more problematic to have an extended family celebration—for sure in a blended family.

Here are some suggestions for connecting with extended families:

- Group picnic in a park
- Backyard barbecue
- Weekend campout or stay at a beach cabin
- Ski trip with a stay at a mountain cabin
- A visit to the state fair with grandkids
- Sporting event
- Dinner at a restaurant with individual families

We have found a wonderful relationship among our siblings. Both of us come from fairly large families, and each side really enjoys being with the other. Shirley's siblings get together from California, Arizona, and Washington State at least once a year. Each family takes a turn fixing a special meal, often from our German Mennonite heritage. It might be watermelon and krullers for breakfast, foul—a Middle Eastern fava bean dish laced with garlic and lemon juice. Northwest salmon, or Armenian specialties from our sister-in-law are some other favorite meals. Though desserts are rare at home, at our get-together, we often top off the meal with other family favorites: cream puffs filled with whipped cream or apricot pie. And of course, we play Mexican Train, a dominoes game—lots of it. As we play, we talk and reminisce, listen to music. The in-laws are sometimes surprised at our stories, or often they've heard them before. We are comfortable together.

Jim's family most every year combines to celebrate a banner year birthday and Christmas. Late spring, most of the Mozenas gather for a weekend campout.

You can imagine at either of our family gatherings with college professors, psychologists, attorneys, teachers, entrepreneurs, a doctor, a politician and even a judge, the conversations we might have. One topic is usually off limits: politics. Of course, there are varied opinions and though we don't agree on everything, we've found siblings to be the most accepting of our marriage.

This is just a snippet of things to consider when you marry for the second or third time. You *will* bring your family with you—whether you're ready or not.

The questionnaire below will help you prepare for challenges involved in blending your two families. Circle your answer to each question as honestly as you can. Take it separately, then share and discuss your answers. Give examples or explanations to assist your partner in fully understanding why you answered as you did and provide details that illustrate your point of view.

Remember, communication is crucial when considering remarriage. There are no right or wrong answers—just clearly communicated and jointly understood issues that can play a significant role in developing a deep and satisfying marriage.

Questionnaire: Yours, Mine, Ours! Blending Families

Issues to consider:

1. I like to spend a lot of time with my children and grand-kids.

1	2	3	4	5	6
Strongly Disagree	Disagree	Somewhat Disagree	Somewhat Agree	Agree	Strongly Agree

2. My children, grandkids, and relatives are a very important part of my life.

1	2	3	4	5	6
Strongly Disagree	Disagree	Somewhat Disagree	Somewhat Agree	Agree	Strongly Agree

3. I like to financially support my kids as the need arises.

1	2	3	4	5	6
Strongly Disagree	Disagree	Somewhat Disagree	Somewhat Agree	Agree	Strongly Agree

4. I like buying gifts for my kids and grandkids and my relatives.

1	2	3	4	5	6
Strongly Disagree	Disagree	Somewhat Disagree	Somewhat Agree	Agree	Strongly Agree

5. I like being involved with kids and grandkids and enjoy attending their various school and sports functions.

1	2	3	4	5	6
Strongly Disagree	Disagree	Somewhat Disagree	Somewhat Agree	Agree	Strongly Agree

6. I believe caring for my elderly parents is an important obligation presently or in the future.

1	2	3	4	5	6
Strongly Disagree	Disagree	Somewhat Disagree	Somewhat Agree	Agree	Strongly Agree

7. I am close to my siblings and it is important for me to maintain a close relationship with them.

1	2	3	4	5	6
Strongly Disagree	Disagree	Somewhat Disagree	Somewhat Agree	Agree	Strongly Agree

There are additional discussion ideas in the appendix.

There's a lot to take in when blending families—even perfect families! Of course, we know no family is perfect—not even the first family, Adam and Eve. There was murder in the first generation and countless rifts in families throughout the Bible: Ishmael and Isaac. Jacob and Esau. King David's blended family had rape and murder mixed in.

Be aware there will be ripples along the way when blending your two lives together. It's good to be proactive and be aware of the red flags when blending your family. Our next chapter continues as we discuss becoming one flesh. Sex. It can be just as special the second or third time around . . .

Chapter Eight ✑

The Touchy Subject: Sex

♪ "The Second Time Around" ♪
Sammy Cahn and Jimmy Van Heusen

From Shirley

*I*t was December 22. A box wrapped with shiny green foil, topped with a large red bow and a tag with my name on it, lay with other presents nestled under the Christmas tree. I shook and touched the carefully wrapped box. What was it? I wasn't sure, but in my eight-year-old heart, I hoped it would be the walking, head-moving doll I'd put on my wish list. That evening, after everyone had gone to bed and the house was quiet, I tiptoed to the tree in the living room that stood front and center and pulled my present out, giving it one last shake. I carefully peeled the scotch tape away and cautiously pulled the paper to one side from the box. I took off the lid, and sure enough, snug in the tissue paper was the doll I'd asked for! There she was, just like the picture in the Sears catalog I'd pored over. It was the Alexandra Doll who turned her head back and forth as she walked, with curly brown hair, bright blue eyes, and a permanent smile on her face. I held her for a moment and then carefully tucked her back into her tissue bed, put on the lid, and wrapped the box once again. Quietly I slipped back into bed. I loved dollies and here was another one to add to my collection.

It was strange though. I was vaguely disappointed. The edge of excitement was gone. Next morning, I felt bad that I hadn't waited until December 24, the day our family opened presents together. There was a strange flatness as I opened the present for the *second* time two days later. The family watched me open the box, waiting to see my expression when I opened my gift. "Ohhhhh," I exclaimed with some false joy, "just what I wanted!" And of course it was. But somehow, the joy was not what it could have been had I waited.

Waiting for the right time brings a fullness of joy. And it's the same with sex before marriage. The Christian worldview says that sex is reserved only for marriage, though our culture does not have a problem with premarital sex. In fact, many couples move in together before they are married and see no hazard in engaging in sex before marriage. Often even Christians turn a blind eye to couples who might be living together before marriage.

Abstaining from sex before marriage is God's idea. I like how *The Message* version in the Bible says it:

> God wants you to live a pure life. Keep yourselves from sexual promiscuity. Learn to appreciate and give dignity to your body, not abusing it, as is so common among those who know nothing of God (1 Thessalonians 4:3–5 MSG).

> Honor marriage and guard the sacredness of sexual intimacy between wife and husband. God draws a firm line against casual and illicit sex (Hebrews 13:4 MSG).

You might ask, "Why wait to have sex? No one will get pregnant. We've already had sex—there won't be any surprises."

Our answer is this: God blesses obedience and it's clearly stated that sex is reserved for marriage.

Jim and I both wished we'd done it differently in our first marriages when we let passion get out of hand before marriage. We each regretted it and wished we had delayed our choices. When couples engage in premarital sex, they are bonding physically and that physical bonding often takes away from the emotional intimacy through exploring each other's personalities and truly getting to know one another. Alice Fryling says: *True intimacy springs from verbal and emotional communion. True intimacy is built on commitment to honesty, love and freedom. True intimacy is not primarily a sexual encounter.*[4]

Some experts report that sexual intimacy short-circuits the emotional bonding process.[5]   What if you didn't wait and now you're stuck with the wrong choices you made? No sexual sin is beyond God's forgiveness. If you first acknowledge you did wrong and ask forgiveness, he'll freely do just that. And then *as far as the east is from the west,* God no longer remembers. That's a promise. And then you put off sex until your marriage. Both Jim and I regretted tremendously not waiting before our first marriages, but we have each in our separate instances realized the wrong and received forgiveness from God.

Jim and I discussed premarital sex on our first date. We openly discussed what the Bible said and believed waiting for sex until marriage was right for us.

---

[4] Alice Fryling, Intervarsity Christian Fellowship of the USA, 1995.
[5] Donald M. Joy,. PhD., *Bonding Relationships in the Image of God* (Evangel Publishing House, 1997).

From Jim

When Shirley and I sat together in the busy coffee shop on our first date, we never stopped talking. We openly discussed many things. I was pleased when she declared, "It may sound a little early, but I should tell you I don't believe in sex before marriage."

"I'm glad you feel that way, because I feel the same way too!" I said with a bit of surprise in my voice—and relief in my soul. I had made mistakes in some of my previous relationships and was glad she had the same opinion of what the Bible said about premarital sex . . .

Our relationship moved very quickly from getting to know each other to being an engaged couple. Early on, in one of our deep conversations, I confessed, "Shirley, there's something you need to know. For a brief time, I was sexually involved with a woman I was dating. I'm deeply ashamed and disappointed in myself for allowing it to happen. I knew it was wrong and I did it anyway. I want you to know that even though I made a terrible mistake once, it won't happen again."

Shirley was intensely quiet for a few moments and then answered, "I can understand how things can get out of hand. Do you regret what happened?"

"Very much."

"Did you ask God to forgive you?"

"Yes. But I still hate it that I allowed it to happen."

"I get it. I wish I hadn't engaged in sex with Bill before marriage either." She sighed and said, "I've regretted it for a long, long time. But then I remind myself what God says about forgiveness. He tells me if I confess I was wrong, he forgives me. With the Holy Spirit's help, I don't plan to make that same mistake again."

"That's me, too. I confessed to God I was wrong and asked him to forgive me. I talked to my pastor about this, and we prayed together about it. He used an example that has stuck with me."

He told me that sex is like a clock. When the clock moves forward, there is no turning the clock backward. Time marches ahead. Like sex. Let's say five or ten minutes after the hour, a couple holds hands. They won't stop holding hands the next time they're together and neither will the clock be moved back. The next step might be a kiss, say, fifteen minutes after the hour. Again the clock won't be turned back and neither will the wonderful expression between sexes—kissing. The more passionate the kissing, the more likely the clock will move forward to petting and touching. The clock cannot be stopped or turned back. Of course, in the analogy used with the clock, the final tick forward would be intercourse. Once that happens, there's no turning back. My pastor reminded me to *Watch the clock, and remember, you can't turn it back.*

It was clear to me and Shirley that we loved each other and were a perfect match. I believed God brought us together. One evening after hours and hours of talking, I leaned over and kissed her lightly on the lips. She returned the kiss, and then said, "When are you going to give me a real kiss?" I immediately responded with a more passionate kiss—one that rocked me to my core.

We were sitting on the couch, facing each other and when we broke away after this kiss, I declared, "I love you, Shirley." I was delighted with her response.

A twinkle in her eye, she said, "I love you too!"

And right then, I knew she was the woman for me. I remembered the vow I'd made when I asked for forgiveness for my past mistakes—that I would not engage in sex before marriage. I remembered my pastor's clock illustration and reminded her, too. "Honey, we have to be careful. This is really hard. You need to help me with this."

"I will," she said.

"I'm going to promise you this: if things get too hot and heavy, I will get up and leave the house."

Shirley smiled and said, "I'm so glad we feel the same way about this. I love and respect you even more because you don't want this to happen again."

Later, we established some boundaries when we were together. We decided we would not engage in passionate kissing. The risk was too great. We remembered the clock couldn't be moved back.

In our marriage ceremony, Pastor Paul Auble was one of the officiants. In his closing remarks he said to us—though more to Jim, *The clock starts now.*

Shortly after we became engaged, we purchased a house together. Jim was ready to make a change and move to my state—he lived in Oregon right across the river from Washington.

We bought the home before we were married, which could have been risky. What if the marriage was called off as happened to Shirley a year and a half earlier? It was only a passing thought, however, for the situation was very different. In our case, we put equal amounts of money down, and the mortgage was in both of our names.

We had the keys to our new home two months before the wedding. That meant a lot of things needed to happen in a short period of time: making needed repairs to the interior and exterior and to the landscaping, selling the home I owned, and moving our possessions to the new home. We planned to have this completed before our wedding. Jim had a house on three acres and a full shop with many things to sell or give away and he was still teaching at the college.

In all of this activity, it seemed like such a timewaster for Jim to drive the forty-five minutes each way to my house every day. Since we had both agreed to wait for sex until after our wedding day, we felt solid in Jim staying overnight in the guest room instead of driving to his home. No more saying goodbye. We were just a room apart at night. Without any real discussion, we now realize this decision was driven by fear. Fear of another loss. Later we realized that somehow sleeping in the same building gave each of us security that the other one wouldn't die.

It sounds crazy, but that's how we thought—until a family member pointed out that even if we were sleeping in separate rooms, it didn't look that way. It appeared we were doing something we didn't believe was right. To our neighbors. Friends or family members who might drop by. Our grandchildren.

This took us aback and we prayed together for guidance. The following day, we made an appointment with our pastor. Before we walked into his office, we sat outside in the car and prayed together, *Lord, we ask You to be with us, and accept whatever Pastor Paul* (Jackson) *has to say.*

Moments later, after telling him about our situation, he pointed out that we were wrong to be staying together in the same house—even if we weren't having sex.

"It's too much of a temptation," he said. "I believe you when you say you aren't having sex—yet. But Jim, you need to make other living arrangements—unless you get married now." We'd already made too many plans to change the wedding date, so we knew what to do.

We thanked our pastor for his bluntly spoken words of wisdom and drove to my house. Within an hour, Jim moved his personal items into the guest room in our future home, still being remodeled.

Secretly, I was relieved, for I never felt that it was right for Jim to stay in the house before we were married. It's true, I had never spoken about this feeling until this meeting. Another important lesson about communication: If Jim had known how I felt, he would not have stayed one night in my house.

There is one last thing to address on this touchy subject. Chemistry. Is it necessary in a relationship with couples who are older? Chemistry is intangible and hard to describe. It is our belief that it's a human emotional desire to be intimate with another person. It is a feeling that makes you want to be with that person all the time. There are butterflies. Sleep doesn't matter.

Though friendship between partners is important, intimacy requires more than just friendship. Sometimes the term used to describe this desire is "honeymoon drugs"—those highly charged endorphins in our brains. Lovers are besotted with each other.

Jim and I experienced those honeymoon drugs before and after our marriage—and our previous ones, too. If there's no chemistry, adjusting to one another could be more difficult when those endorphins wear off, usually between eighteen and thirty-six months. We have no doubt that chemistry is important. Usually, it is obvious when dating; if you are aware you don't have chemistry, perhaps you should proceed cautiously in your plans to marry this person. This takes an honest discussion with your potential mate and most importantly: yourself.

If you had a fulfilling marriage with a healthy sex life, you know it is important in the life of a marriage. We can tell you, it *can* happen again. You don't have to give up chemistry because you're of a certain age.

When you are married, what's sex like after sixty? We can tell you it's different than when we were younger. Yet it is still exciting, sometimes dramatic, and fulfilling. You may find it isn't as often or as urgent, however.

The man and the woman may have physical limitations. Talk to your physician about those limitations before marriage and discuss them with each other as well. That can prevent any surprises or disappointment the first time you are sexually intimate together.

Sex in seasoned citizens is nearly as important as in younger adults. It is a myth that men and women lose their ability to perform sexually after a certain age. The reality is you can still have a satisfying sex life. Would either partner be willing to pleasure the other if one cannot perform the sex act? Communication about what to do if this is the case is essential—before and after marriage. There are many ways to express intimacy in marriage besides the sex act. It might be a massage. A bath together. A couple *can* pleasure each other without intercourse. It still can be an intimate event. Sex doesn't have to be boring when you get older. It is as good as you make it.[6]

Sex is one of God's good gifts. Right from the beginning, marriage and intimacy was God's idea. In Genesis God instructed Adam and Eve, "That is why a man leaves his father and mother and is united with his wife, and they become one flesh" (Genesis 2:24 NIV). Song of Solomon extols the pleasures of sexual intimacy and the joys of marriage explicitly throughout the book. Intimacy in marriage maintains the special bond of closeness, connectedness, and communication. We think the "honeymoon drugs" are good too!

Will there be any comparisons of sex from our previous marriages? There shouldn't be. For both of us, we consider the past the past and are confident in our mates and our love and that special chemistry for each other. We are exclusive in each other's heart and it will remain so until death.

The questionnaire below will help you examine differences and similarities in the way you view sex. You're guaranteed to have stimulating conversation! Circle your answer to each question. Take it separately, then share and discuss your answers. Give examples or

---

[6] https://www.health.harvard.edu/staying-healthy/attitudes-about-sexuality-and-aging.

explanations to assist your partner in fully understanding why you answered as you did and provide details that illustrate your point of view.

Remember, communication is crucial when considering remarriage. There are no right or wrong answers—just clearly communicated and jointly understood issues that can play a significant role in developing a deep and satisfying marriage.

Questionnaire: The Touchy Subject: Sex

Issues to consider:

1. I believe in abstaining from sex until after marriage.

1	2	3	4	5	6
Strongly Disagree	Disagree	Somewhat Disagree	Somewhat Agree	Agree	Strongly Agree

2. I have determined a specific point or boundary where I feel comfortable with physical intimacy (holding hands, kissing, petting and touch) before we are married.

1	2	3	4	5	6
Strongly Disagree	Disagree	Somewhat Disagree	Somewhat Agree	Agree	Strongly Agree

3. We have discussed what our physical/sexual boundaries are.

1	2	3	4	5	6
Strongly Disagree	Disagree	Somewhat Disagree	Somewhat Agree	Agree	Strongly Agree

4. It is both our responsibility to maintain those boundaries.

1	2	3	4	5	6
Strongly Disagree	Disagree	Somewhat Disagree	Somewhat Agree	Agree	Strongly Agree

5. There is chemistry between us.

1	2	3	4	5	6
Strongly Disagree	Disagree	Somewhat Disagree	Somewhat Agree	Agree	Strongly Agree

6. I have clearly communicated my expectations regarding sex after marriage (frequency, who initiates, etc).

1	2	3	4	5	6
Strongly Disagree	Disagree	Somewhat Disagree	Somewhat Agree	Agree	Strongly Agree

7. We have discussed each of our desires regarding sex after marriage.

| 1 | 2 | 3 | 4 | 5 | 6 |

| Strongly Disagree | Disagree | Somewhat Disagree | Somewhat Agree | Agree | Strongly Agree |

There are additional discussion ideas found in the appendix.

We've discussed sex after mid-life. There is passion through-out life and yes, at any age, chemistry is important. We discussed boundaries that should be taken before marriage. After marriage, there should be accommodations for physical limitations and communication about them. There must be open communication about sex during marriage—regardless of how many years a couple has been married and how old they are. We've also concluded that sex after sixty can be fulfilling and exciting, too.

We're a little more than halfway through the book. Put on your seat belts, because we're going to discuss health and end-of-life is-sues. Not a comfortable topic, but so very necessary!

Be sure to listen to the song beforehand. It will give you hope.

Chapter Nine ✑

In Sickness and in Health—Can You Say Those Vows?

♪ "There Will Be A Day" ♪
Jeremy Camp

We all deal with health issues throughout our lives, but as we age, health is a much larger issue. Before marrying again, you really need to consider what might happen later. One of you will get sick. One of you may die before the other, and death could be a result of a challenging and heartbreaking illness. There are risks in meeting and marrying, regardless of age. We encourage you to not rush your situation. Talk to God, he's there all the time, he can reveal to you what his will is. That's a promise. "If any of you lacks wisdom, you should ask God, who gives generously to all without finding fault, and it will be given to you" (James 1:5 NIV).

One of our dear friends said her final goodbye to her much-loved spouse recently. We hurt for her because we have an idea of what she's going through. This is the second time she's experienced the loss of a husband.

When Ellen and Tim had married, they were in their late sixties. About seven years earlier, they both lost a spouse to cancer. Two years later, a mutual friend introduced Tim and Ellen to each other and soon they knew there was love. Three months later, they were married with a joy-filled ceremony, all their children in attendance.

They were so happy. Ellen was a giddy bride filled with joy she'd found love again. Tim was no different. They delighted in each other.

Together they learned to do new things. Ellen had never camped or gone fishing, but Tim showed her how much fun it would be, and sure enough, Ellen liked it! They did some traveling and fit into each other's lives and those of their families easily, as if they'd known each other a lifetime.

They combined households and moved into Ellen's home. They built a shop to store their outdoor equipment where Tim tinkered and did woodwork. Tim became a member at Ellen's church, and they traveled to visit family in other parts of the United States.

Four years passed. Near Christmastime, Tim developed some worrisome health symptoms. After many tests that Tim insisted on, it turned out to be stomach cancer—the same as his first wife, Linda.

The next few months were hazardous, with visits to the hospital emergency room and waiting to be admitted. Discomfort. Relief from the discomfort. And tests revealing that surgery didn't take away the cancer completely.

Tim and Ellen knew they might not have much more time together, so while they still could travel, they did. They camped places they'd been before: at the beach they'd come to love and still could really enjoy it.

Then they stayed closer to home and doctors. Tim didn't stop living. He kept mowing the lawn and working in his shop. But after some time, he didn't have the strength to do those things and he did more resting. Ellen had taken excellent care of him. Family drew around them, and some from out of town stayed with them to say their goodbyes.

Tim had a firm faith in his Savior, Jesus, and seemed unafraid of dying. He was ready. But his family and wife weren't quite ready to let him go.

He was a strong man. He went weeks without nourishment and eventually without water since his stomach wouldn't tolerate food or drink. But he didn't complain.

We visited them several times during Tim's illness. Even while painfully ill, he was always upbeat. His eyes had a sparkle. He continued to assure us he was ready to meet Jesus. Four days before his death we saw him for the last time. He was now in bed and on pain medications, but still lucid and even talked with us lightheartedly about what it would be like to meet Jesus. We sat on the big bed with Tim lying down on one side, Jim and I seated on the other side. Ellen sat in a nearby chair.

Five years earlier when she'd told me she was engaged to be married, others asked if she was fearful she'd lose him as she had lost Don, her first husband. She countered with, "Why would you say 'no thank you' when such a gift is offered to you?" She accepted Tim's invitation to marry him and spend the rest of their days together. They had nearly five years, four happy and healthy ones.

We prayed together that last time we saw Tim. We told him we'd see him later—on the other side. On that last visit, when saying goodbye to Ellen at the front door, I asked her, "Are you sorry you married again, only to have to say goodbye?" I felt I could ask this because we'd both lost husbands in death before.

She understood because she said quite easily, "Loving someone hurts; it's a risk we all take. I don't like it, but I'm not sorry. It was and is worth the joy."

In early fall, two months before their fifth wedding anniversary, Tim passed into eternity.

It won't be easy for Ellen. She knows it. I know it—both of us were where she is, mourning her husband. But she won't be alone. She'll have the Blessed Comforter right beside her. She'll need her family and friends, but most of all, she has Jesus. There are no guarantees for continuing good health.

When Jim and I met, both of us were hale and hearty. I hiked and loved the outdoors. I exercised at the gym at least three times weekly. Jim was a runner and ran five miles on the rural roads near his home three times a week. We both were interested in eating healthy and keeping physically fit. I was more interested in hiking and camping than Jim was, but he was willing to learn. Together we climbed Mt. St. Helens with my daughter, Erika, her two sons, and some of her friends.

During our three-month engagement, we openly discussed our health and the medications we were prescribed. Niggling thoughts of fear ran through my mind. *What if Jim has an aneurysm like Blair did? What if he dies before we get married? What if? What then?* Jim had fear too.

After eighteen months of marriage, we experienced our first major health issue with a simple act of taking four steps up into our RV.

From Shirley

It was a beautiful late spring evening at Cape Lookout State Park, a popular Oregon beach campground. "I'll be right back," I said. We'd been enjoying sumptuous fresh seafood we'd picked up from the dock. We were sitting around a cozy campfire and having a lively discussion with Jim's sister Rosaleen and brother-in-law Ron. I went to retrieve something from our RV and dashed through the screen of trees to our adjoining campsite. It had been an unusually beautiful late spring day at the beach. We hiked high above the cape, snapping calendar-perfect photos of the Pacific Ocean far below.

I bolted up the first two steps of the RV, peering inside, not wanting our cat to escape. As I leaned forward and took the next step, I tripped and fell the few feet down. Pain seared up my leg as my ankle turned, and I knew I'd done serious damage. I looked at my left ankle and saw it was bent in an abnormal angle. My first thought was *I'm not going to be able to hike again!* I'd just finished being laid up with surgery on my right foot, and now this!

"Jim!" I cried out. No response. "Jim!" I called again. Two women walking by the campsite asked if they could help. "Ask my husband to come over," I pleaded. Moments later, Jim stood by my side along with Ron and Rosaleen. "I did it this time," I moaned.

"Oh, honey," Jim said. He knelt behind me, holding me up. My foot flopped crookedly and I was afraid to move it. Rosaleen quickly found ice to place on the injury.

A park ranger cautioned us, "Tillamook Hospital is about ten miles away. You should have your ankle checked."

I leaned back against Jim's chest. My head was spinning, and I told myself, *Hold on. Don't black out.* I was going into shock and I knew that would make it worse. After a quick decision, Ron brought his truck over to our campsite and they carefully loaded me into the cab with my foot propped up, wrapped in a towel and ice.

After viewing the X-rays, the ER doctor told us surgery would be necessary. "You have an unsupported break and it will need hardware."

We discussed options: there was a competent orthopedic surgeon on staff, but no operating room available for two days. Several phone calls later, we decided to return the one hundred miles to our hometown where a surgeon would perform surgery on my left ankle. I looked up at Jim, tears rolling down my cheeks. I was scared—and frustrated. Jim hugged me and patted my hand. "It'll be all right. I love you. We'll get through this," he said.

Somehow, Jim and a nurse helped me into the RV and up onto

the four-foot high bed. The RV van rumbled on in the darkness. The two-hour trip seemed to take forever. I lay twenty feet behind the driver's seat and could hear the occasional *prrrp, prrrp, prrrp* of our tires hitting the traffic buttons on the lane markers. "Are you awake up there?" I called worriedly. I was scared Jim would fall asleep and we'd crash with my already injured body.

"I'm wide awake and full of adrenaline. I won't fall asleep!" he assured me.

At the hospital, Dr. Coale proposed a plan. "Your ankle won't be able to bear any weight for at least six weeks," he said.

Jim held my hand and kissed me goodbye as they wheeled me into the OR. "Did you call Erika and Todd (my kids)?" I asked. I was a little frightened, but also knew my ankle—and my life for that matter—were in God's hands. I wished I could re-do that fateful evening and somehow avoid the fall from the RV step. The OR nurse distracted me by asking lots of questions when she found out I was an author. Soon I was asleep from anesthesia

After the surgery, Dr. Coale explained to Jim that because of my osteoporosis, the break had looked like a fall from a tall building. "We put her ankle back together," he reported. "We used seven screws, one plate, and several pins."

Two days later, I was back home. I felt so helpless! And some self-pity, too. *Why did this have to happen to me?* As I sat in the recliner, I told myself this wasn't a surprise to God. He knew before it ever happened that there would be no surgeon available in the small hospital at Tillamook. He knew the perfect physician—as it turned out, a specialist and nationally recognized vascular surgeon—who could put my ankle back together.

I was groggy with pain meds and limited to a walker and a wheelchair. Jim had his hands full. Friends brought meals, lent crutches, and commiserated. It took every ounce of energy I had to go to the bathroom in the walker and my hop-scoot routine was exhausting. *How do elderly people do this?* I didn't believe I was elderly but wondered as I huffed and puffed to accomplish minimal personal hygiene, brushing my teeth and hair and showering, with help from Jim. Nothing was easy. I feared for my future. Would I be normal again? I didn't want to worry and pushed my anxious thoughts away.

Our trip to Disneyland with one of our daughters and her four-kid family was to take place in two weeks. Would I be able to do it? I wasn't sure. "Let's take it a day at a time," Jim said. "We'll decide just before if we can go."

Three days before our planned departure date, we decided I could do it if perched in the rear of the RV up on the bed. During our vacation, I discovered that sitting in a wheelchair was just as tiring as walking—maybe more so.

In spite of my limitations, we had a great time in the world-famous amusement park. Each grandkid helped to push my wheelchair and I even went on some rides—wheelchairs take first priority, an advantage I hadn't counted on!

Seven weeks after my surgery, I became more independent, using a knee scooter to move around. Simple household tasks—such as watering plants, cooking meals, or shopping—remained a challenge. By the end of each day, I grew tired and frustrated that I couldn't do things as quickly as before my accident. Navigating carefully through the house and yard was tiresome but I reminded myself that some are bound to wheelchairs for the entirety of their lives.

By week ten I began walking with a boot cast and crutch. I was grateful for Jim and his patience with me. I appreciated each grandchild who willingly pushed my chair or ran to fetch things for me. There was my extended family who prayed for me and cheered me on.

As the Apostle Paul said in Philippians 4:11 (NIV), "I have learned to be content whatever the circumstances." That is our goal. Keep in mind sometimes recovery will be different. I was blessed with circumstances where my ankle healed nicely. Sometimes that doesn't happen.

From Jim

For most of my adult life, I have battled Generalized Anxiety Disorder (GAD). Throughout the years, I have occasionally seen a counselor to address symptoms. I've been on medication for years, but I maintained a very active and productive career as a business owner, life with my family, and activity in church life as an elder and fulfilling service in children's ministry.

There have been times when the GAD seemed to be higher than other times. We were scheduled to take a thirty-day cruise a few years ago, from Seattle, Washington, to Sydney, Australia. For whatever reason, my GAD really acted up.

"We need to talk," I told Shirley.

"What's wrong? she asked, folding some shorts and T-shirts and placing them in her suitcase, packing for our five-week trip.

"I don't think I can make it."

"What do you mean, make it?"

"Our trip. I can't explain it. I'm just feeling very overwhelmed. There's this dread hanging over me. I can't get it out of my mind that something bad might happen. What if I go nuts in the middle of the Pacific Ocean? What can the ship doctor do for me?"

Shirley didn't know what to say or do to calm my fears, but answered, "I'm willing to cancel our trip if you think that will help. Don't we have travel insurance?"

"Let me call Tonia (our travel agent). Let's see what she says about canceling."

"How about calling the doctor, too? Maybe he can prescribe something different."

I made some phone calls and an appointment with my physician. "Tonia says the travel insurance doesn't cover this type of illness."

Frustrated and angry, Shirley said, "What? I thought that's why we have insurance!"

We talked and prayed, and with the doctor's blessing, we decided we should not cancel the trip. "I think I'll be okay," I said. "I wish I didn't have to deal with this. I can't even explain it!" I said, shaking my head in frustration.

We sailed out of Seattle on a blustery October morning and the trip went without a hitch. We enjoyed a wonderful cruise— the captain remarked he'd never experienced such a smooth Pacific crossing. We met new people, enjoyed tempting foods, took dance classes, and enjoyed dreamy sunsets. We lolled on warm beaches during port calls as we sailed to Sydney. When we arrived in Sydney at sunrise, the Sydney Opera House was right there! It's one of those unforgettable views that leaves you breathless. We were cruising slowly, so we had many minutes to snap photos.

We disembarked from the ship, obtained rooms in The Rocks district, and explored even more of the beautiful city of Sydney.

The feelings of overwhelming dread I experienced earlier dissipated.

The following summer was uneventful, except late in the season, the GAD symptoms worsened. Worse than they'd ever been. My physician continued to try new medications, but nothing seemed to help. I began to suffer Parkinson-like symptoms.

"Jim, I don't like how your body is acting. Do you think it might be the meds you're taking?" Shirley asked me with concern.

"Paul noticed I've got some strange symptoms, too," I said. Paul was my walking buddy and a close friend. Our friendship ran deep and when something concerned either of us, we honestly told each other.

After checking the side effects of the meds I was on, we realized we needed to consult another doctor. Getting an appointment with a renowned psychiatrist in Portland within days was a miracle. This doctor listened to us, observed my symptoms, reviewed my medications, and said, "You need to get off all these pills." He shook his head with concern, saying "You are over-medicated. It might be your symptoms are a side effect." He prescribed one only, similar to one of the four I was taking, gave me his cell number, and told me to call him if I needed to. After a few adjustments of medication, I began to feel better.

We believe a conversation with an acquaintance from out of town was a nudging from the Holy Spirit. We regularly have lunch with Marlen. He asked how he could pray for us, and we told him about the GAD acting up. He said he would pray but also told us how his daughter-in-law was trying a new treatment called *neurofeedback*. "It's not normally covered by insurance, but it might be worth a try," he said.

I investigated with the help of a website and found the clinic that performed the neurofeedback in our area and made arrangements to give the treatments a try. [7]

Right after that conversation with Marlen, I began investigating and easily found a clinic in Portland. "Do you think I should do this?" I asked Shirley.

"I don't care if the insurance doesn't cover the cost. It's worth it to give it a try."

The next day, I made my first appointment and immediately afterward saw some results. With each visit, I felt even better.

---

[7] http://bit.ly/2tXFYPJ.

We are grateful for the improvement in my mental health, but there are no guarantees there will not be another hurdle to overcome or live with.

If you are considering marriage, end of life and/or terminal illness must be discussed. Accidents and illness happen. We are reminded with each passing year we are getting older and know there's an end point. Often couples ignore the part of those wedding vows "'til death do us part." Just as with Tim and Ellen, one of you may enter eternity before the other. One of you may have a chronic illness with complications that lead to death like Shirley's husband Bill. Or one of you may have a heart attack or brain aneurysm that quickly takes your life, like Shirley's husband Blair. Jim's wife Kathy died of a long-term illness.

Discussions of treatment, chemotherapy, and other life-saving treatment need to be considered. Kathy did not want to attempt a lung transplant or be a guinea pig for new medications. She realized most likely there would be little benefit. After two years, she was placed on hospice. It is helpful to have a discussion before an illness takes place. Some people are adamant they won't have chemotherapy or surgery.

While you may sometimes prefer to visit your doctors alone, it might be good for your mate to come with you to an office call—especially an urgent/emergency visit. Often it's a good idea so the other person can ask questions as well as having an extra set of ears to hear what the doctor says.

Another discussion that should take place in the event of death is where does your loved one want to have their body placed? Will you be cremated or in a burial plot? Do you already have a burial plot, or a niche in a columbarium already purchased? Shirley's experience confirms the importance of such a conversation . . .

"It's a good time to organize our financial files," Blair said.

"When do you think we'll finish combining everything?" I asked, looking at the sea of paper. We were tying up loose ends of our marriage and reviewing important documents including our wills.

"I don't know," shrugged Blair. "But there's no hurry. We have plenty of time."

I picked up a document and turned the pages. "You'll be buried next to Wisha (Blair's wife Patricia), it says here," I mused. "At the plot in Walla Walla." It wasn't news to me, but there were details we needed to clarify.

"My name is already on the headstone," said Blair, not looking up.

"Yes. And your wedding date. December . . . what was it?"

"December 23, 1972," said Blair, leaning back on the couch pillows. I stood by, holding out the pages of the document.

Blair glanced at me, bit his lip, then with resolution reached over and clicked off the television. "It has already been decided," he said. "You'll be buried next to Bill. I'll be with Wisha."

Our voices were low, serious. There was tension in the brightly lit room. A starry night sky showed through the high windows.

"I know," I said carefully. "I understand why you need to be buried next to her. You're keeping your promise to Wisha. But I feel left out. What about *our* marriage? Is that to go unmentioned?"

Carefully, reasonably, we continued our discussion, keeping our voices level, doing our best to state our points of view and listen to the other. "We do need to acknowledge that we had children with our first mates," said Blair, folding his hands together. "It makes sense that we should honor that union."

"Yes," I agreed, dropping onto the couch next to him. "But shouldn't we include our own marriage covenant?"

Blair tilted his head to the side thoughtfully. "Yes," he said. "But how?"

As we talked, we came up with a plan. Blair's headstone would include the following: *Married Shirley Mae Rudberg on August 16, 2008.*

"I would be honored to have your name at my final resting place," said Blair, and gently reached out and squeezed my hand. I smiled with relief, my tension eased . . . Little did we know Blair would die suddenly less than a month later.

Since that time nine years ago, my name has changed again. My burial plans are the same: My plot is next to my first husband, Bill. It's in the cemetery where my parents are buried, where the headstone of my third child is placed next to her daddy. On my headstone, I wish for all my names to be inscribed. Each last name has meaning and were chapters in my life: Quiring, my maiden name, Rudberg, the name of my first husband and father to my children, Bill; Graybill, the name of my second husband, Blair; and Mozena, the name I took when I married Jim.

Jim wishes to be cremated and will have his ashes interred in the cemetery where his parents and siblings are buried. We had a lively discussion regarding his burial site one afternoon while writing this section of the book.

"That's great that you want to be buried at Mount Calvary with your family. Please keep in mind I most likely won't be able to visit the site very often if you are the first to go," I said. "It's on the other side of Portland. Who knows if I'm even able to drive then?"

"I think it would be good if I was near my family."

We talked over the next few days and visited the cemetery, purchased a niche in the columbarium. We concluded if I needed help in transportation to visit Jim's final resting spot, family members would be willing to help me. We are relieved both of our final arrangements for burial are made.

We have no idea when either of us will have to put into place these wishes, but we have discussed them. We need to add this to our final wishes in our last will and testament as well.

Just as sitting in an attorney's office to complete your last will and testament is not comfortable, neither is discussing funeral plans. But if you choose to love again after you've already lost one mate in death or divorce, these plans must be made. It makes it so much easier for your spouse and family if you have it written down, preferably in a will. And you will be glad those plans are completed.

Even with these uncomfortable discussions, we are not sorry to experience the second chance we both experienced—not once, not twice, and for Shirley, three times. We are grateful.

Jim explains, when people ask him how he can love again, "When I loved Kathy, it was as much as I had the capacity to love. After she died, I was scrubbed with pain and loss, and because of the pain and loss, I had more capacity to love someone else."

If you choose to love and remarry, remember the vows you'll say: "'til death do us part." It is likely one of you will leave this earth at some unknown time before the other. Some people choose not to accept this risk of loss, and they remain single. That of course is their decision.

Jim also learned to be content in his singleness. After his early engagement to the wrong person, he realized he needed to work through his grief and be content with himself. He did a major remodel on his home and considered selling it and making a fresh start in a place with less yard upkeep. He was available for his young grandkids and enjoyed accompanying them on school field trips, working in the classroom, and attending basketball tournaments.

He took spiritual retreats and asked God to help him know what his will for his life might be.

It's important when you're considering remarriage to be open and honest about any health conditions you may be experiencing. No surprises! Life has enough on its own. The questionnaire below will help you start that discussion and perhaps think of scenarios that would never occur to you. Take the quiz separately, then share and discuss your answers. Give examples or explanations to assist your partner in fully understanding why you answered as you did and provide details that illustrate your point of view. Circle your answer to each question.

Remember, communication is crucial when considering remarriage. There are no right or wrong answers—just clearly communicated and jointly understood issues that can play a significant role in developing a deep and satisfying marriage.

Questionnaire: In Sickness and in Health—Can You Say Those Vows?

Issues to Consider:

1. I have shared all major medical conditions or health issues I have had in my lifetime.

1	2	3	4	5	6
Strongly Disagree	Disagree	Somewhat Disagree	Somewhat Agree	Agree	Strongly Agree

2. I have disclosed all the medications I am currently taking.

1	2	3	4	5	6
Strongly Disagree	Disagree	Somewhat Disagree	Somewhat Agree	Agree	Strongly Agree

3. I have shared all health-related issues I am currently experiencing.

1	2	3	4	5	6
Strongly Disagree	Disagree	Somewhat Disagree	Somewhat Agree	Agree	Strongly Agree

4. Staying physically fit is very important to me.

1	2	3	4	5	6
Strongly Disagree	Disagree	Somewhat Disagree	Somewhat Agree	Agree	Strongly Agree

5. I pay a lot of attention to my diet and nutrition.

1	2	3	4	5	6
Strongly Disagree	Disagree	Somewhat Disagree	Somewhat Agree	Agree	Strongly Agree

6. I would appreciate if my spouse accompanies me to doctor visits.

1	2	3	4	5	6
Strongly Disagree	Disagree	Somewhat Disagree	Somewhat Agree	Agree	Strongly Agree

7. I have made specific plans on where I would like to be buried and the method. Cremation or traditional burial.

1	2	3	4	5	6
Strongly Disagree	Disagree	Somewhat Disagree	Somewhat Agree	Agree	Strongly Agree

8. I have developed written "advance directives" so that others know my wishes at my end of life. (Search the internet for many sample forms of advance directives for your state.)

1	2	3	4	5	6
Strongly Disagree	Disagree	Somewhat Disagree	Somewhat Agree	Agree	Strongly Agree

9. I believe there are many benefits to alternative medical approaches, i.e. vitamin supplements, chiropractic, and naturopathic approaches to healing and healthcare.

1	2	3	4	5	6
Strongly Disagree	Disagree	Somewhat Disagree	Somewhat Agree	Agree	Strongly Agree

10. Some states have laws regarding "death with dignity," where physician-assisted dying are allowed.[8] This is something I would consider.

1	2	3	4	5	6
Strongly Disagree	Disagree	Somewhat Disagree	Somewhat Agree	Agree	Strongly Agree

There are additional discussion ideas in the appendix.

We've discussed how we will face health issues throughout our lives, but more so as we grow older. There should be discussion of current health issues each of you may be experiencing, and what the outcome might be. We discussed what type of health care would be desired if one of you becomes critically ill. We also discussed funeral and burial plans and where you want to be buried.

---

[8] https://bit.ly/3bdkONO.

A person's choice of medical care and end-of-life issues might be painful to discuss, but even more divisive is the area of politics. Read on.

Chapter Ten ✑

Politics: Can We Be Civil?

♪ "God Bless the U.S.A." ♪
Lee Greenwood

Some people rarely pay attention to politics until it's time to vote, if they even vote. However, if you are even mildly interested in whom you'd vote for, and what your party platforms are, you most likely would want to be in the same party. It's more peaceful if you share similar political values.

From Jim

Earlier, in chapter 4, I disclosed my relationship with Darlene. It grew very tricky when we discussed politics. One evening, as I was preparing to cook some steaks for dinner, I suggested, "How about we put on Fox News while we wait for the grill to warm up?"

"I absolutely will not have that station come into my home!" Darlene said, shaking her head with emphasis. "I don't agree with anything they say or report."

I knew we hadn't voted for the same presidential candidate in the last election, but I hadn't realized how strongly she felt about politics until then. That encounter told me we were on opposite ends of the political spectrum: she was extremely liberal, and I was conservative. Earlier we had believed our relationship would work by ignoring politics and simply being companions, but we found that not to be true.

I began to believe we would not be compatible, so this incident made it clear that our relationship most likely wouldn't work. Soon after this, we parted ways.

From Shirley

The first time I was looking for a match in 2008, I thought mutual views on politics were important in a relationship because I had always been interested in politics. Currently, it is even more important to share similar political beliefs with your partner because of the acrimony in our politics—nationally and locally.

Both of us are from families that have diverse political opinions. And on both sides of our families, we've had to establish an unspoken rule to not discuss politics. They've been too divisive.

There are, however, some couples who've successfully found a way to be politically opposed and maintain at least the appearance of a happy marriage. One well known couple who have done this is Mary Matalin and James Carville. He is a staunch Democratic party strategist who helped Bill Clinton get elected. She is a Libertarian Republican strategist and worked for Ronald Reagan, George H.W. Bush, and George W. Bush.

Carville says, "It's a learning process. Sometimes, you just have to understand you are going to disagree. You're not going to change anybody's mind so why talk about it? You just have to let things go."

In the Naples Daily News, Carville and Matalin confess their secret is to compartmentalize their lives. Politics is just one part of the household picture. In Matalin's brief bio, she says, "We do not talk politics at home."[9]

Jim has a very close friend who is on the opposite side of the political spectrum. This is his friend Paul, who noticed some physical changes in Jim that concerned Paul and he mentioned them to Jim. Their friendship has spanned more than thirty years. Paul was with Jim when his wife Kathy was dying. He was with Jim when he was involved with a woman Paul didn't believe was right for Jim. When they are both in town, they set aside Friday mornings to walk together and have coffee at a nearby Starbucks. They have mutually agreed to not talk politics. Sometimes, one of them might ask permission to discuss a certain issue, and the other has the option to go ahead with the discussion or not. But for the most part, politics is taboo. It has worked—but they aren't married either!

Even though a couple with opposing political views might be able to keep their marriage together by keeping that area of their lives closed off to their spouse, there are biblical reasons for avoiding this complication.

> "Do not become partners with those who do not believe, for what partnership is there between righteousness and lawlessness, or what fellowship does light have with darkness?" (2 Corinthians 7:14 NET).

> "Can two walk together unless they are agreed?" (Amos 3:3 NKJ).

It's our recommendation, as observers of the human race and based on our understanding of God's Word, that it's better for couples to have similar political beliefs. Why set yourself up for some-

---

[9] http://bit.ly/2XmAIzf.

thing that most likely would bring division and potentially interfere with your intellectual intimacy? You have to consider whether the tension and disagreement that might ensue are worth the risk.

The questionnaire below will help you broach the subject of the role politics will play in your potential union. Circle your answer to each question. Take it separately, then share and discuss your answers. Give examples or explanations to assist your partner in fully understanding why you answered as you did and provide details that illustrate your point of view.

Remember, communication is crucial when considering remarriage. There are no right or wrong answers—just clearly communicated and jointly understood issues that can play a significant role in developing a deep and satisfying marriage.

Questionnaire: Politics: Can We Be Civil?

Issues to consider:

1. Politics are very important to me.

1	2	3	4	5	6
Strongly Disagree	Disagree	Somewhat Disagree	Somewhat Agree	Agree	Strongly Agree

2. Sharing my political party and agreeing on the platform is important to me.

1	2	3	4	5	6
Strongly Disagree	Disagree	Somewhat Disagree	Somewhat Agree	Agree	Strongly Agree

3. I enjoy watching cable news and/or listening to talk radio.

1	2	3	4	5	6
Strongly Disagree	Disagree	Somewhat Disagree	Somewhat Agree	Agree	Strongly Agree

4. I enjoy political discussions with my mate.

1	2	3	4	5	6
Strongly Disagree	Disagree	Somewhat Disagree	Somewhat Agree	Agree	Strongly Agree

5. I have core beliefs that are very important to me, such as: pro-life or pro-choice, monogamous marriage, and homosexuality.

1	2	3	4	5	6
Strongly Disagree	Disagree	Somewhat Disagree	Somewhat Agree	Agree	Strongly Agree

There are additional discussion ideas found in the appendix.

We've discussed how politics can be divisive and though some couples have had a successful marriage with differing politics, it's a better idea to be similar in your political beliefs.

We've covered the seven areas to consider before marriage. There's one more area. You might be surprised how it can affect your relationship.

Chapter Eleven ∽

Quotidian

♪ "You Don't Bring Me Flowers" ♪
Neil Diamond/Alan Bergman

*T*here's a multisyllable word describing day-to-day routines that have significant effect on our lives together: quotidian. The issues we've discussed in previous chapters are extensive and require careful consideration. But the quotidian can also have an important effect on your relationship and may actually also be a deal breaker. These issues can produce irritation or discomfort that might make living together a strain or even worse.

Are you a mess-y or a clean-y? Does it matter? As a fairly neat person (not as neat as some I know), it would be a deal breaker to live with someone who never picked up after themselves.

Would you rather live in the city or in the country? Would you prefer a condo in an urban area where you could walk to movies and restaurants? Or would you rather live in the suburbs or in the country with few nearby neighbors?

How about eating styles? For me, meals are very important, and time should be taken in planning and preparing them. Having a family meal together is important. All my siblings enjoy preparing and eating a good meal with a fine wine. Jim's side is not so much that way. That's all right though, as long as both are willing to participate most of the time. Do you like to set the table with matching plates, or would you prefer eating on a tray in front of the TV? Are you willing to occasionally pay good money for a dinner in a fine restaurant or is fast food just as enjoyable?

Do you like to stay home most of the time, or would you be willing to travel? Would you be willing to be a snowbird? Or would you hate leaving your family who might live in the area for even a few months? Do you have a fear of flying or of ocean cruises?

How about normal day-to-day chores? Do you pick up after yourself? Put your soiled clothes into a hamper? Would you expect your spouse to do all the laundry? Are you willing to share closet space with your spouse? Do you close the cupboard doors when you open them? Do you empty the dishwasher when it needs to be emptied? Do you like to work in the garden and clean the yard or are you okay with your spouse doing it all? Does one of you have a preference to hire a handyman instead of do-it-yourself, assuming one of you has the appropriate skills?

What recreational activities do you enjoy? Monday night football—or all day Sunday? I have family members who never miss a game—and others who hate the sound of the crowd that fills the room with "noise." Would you enjoy going to a baseball game or a NASCAR race? Live theatre or ballet?

How set are you in your ways? Are you willing to help out in the kitchen? Do you like to cook? Jim is a willing helper, though he doesn't initiate much cooking himself. He's willing to pinch hit if I'm not feeling well or don't feel like cooking. Are you willing to share household tasks? Together, Jim and I clean our house on Mondays if we're home. He does all the vacuuming. I do the bathrooms (except his), dusting, perking the kitchen up to my standards.

How about nighttime habits? Do you like to go to bed early and rise before the sun comes up? Or are you a late-to-bed person who loves to watch movies late into the evening? Is this a deal breaker? Probably not, but combined with other differences, it might be.

Hobbies. Do you have similar likes and dislikes? Do you enjoy going to the gym, hiking, camping, walking, reading, watching movies? What kind of music do you enjoy? I love jazz and classical music. Jim enjoys some country and classical. We compromise on what we listen to. For Christmas this year, Jim gifted me with tickets to Michael Bublé, not his favorite vocal artist, but one of mine. He's willing to compromise and enjoy the concert—even though he'd prefer a Alan Jackson or a Sarah Brightman concert. Gratefully, we both enjoy having the classical station on in the car. There's always room for compromise.

If you've been widowed or divorced, is it safe to bring up that person's name or memory? Would you be comfortable discussing your past and your mate's past? In our marriage, both of our previous spouses are now deceased, and we freely talk about them. Jim talks more about his late wife Kathy than his divorced wife.

Feeling free to bring up those memories is a very real area to consider. Given the significance of memories that have shaped who we are as persons, this is an issue that may be more significant than some of the others in this chapter.

What about friends? Are you willing to become part of your spouse's network of friends? Are you willing to make new friendships to establish your own network?

We talked about blending families in an earlier chapter. What about blending your household? Are you open to purchasing a home together or to moving into either of your homes? In our case, we both sold our homes, combined all our household goods and then started donating a lot of stuff to our kids or charity. It was exciting having a fresh new start with a home we bought together. In my second marriage I moved into Blair's home. Although he was very open to anything I wanted to change, it never truly felt like it was my home but something temporary. I know I wouldn't feel that way if something happened to Jim and I was alone in the home we purchased together. We know of couples who did move into one or the other homes, and it was fine. It is really a personal choice, yet one that needs to be addressed.

I learned in my first marriage that it was all right to not win the argument. Jim learned the same principle. It took many years, however, to figure that out. Because of those lessons learned, it isn't a problem in our marriage now. How important is it for you to win an argument? Can you identify things about which you are not willing to compromise, or to "lose"? The discussions you have after answering the questions in the previous chapters may help you to answer that question.

The questionnaire below will help you identify areas of everyday life that might pose challenges to your relationship. Circle your answer to each question as honestly as you can. Take it separately, then share and discuss your answers. Give examples or explanations to assist your partner in fully understanding why you answered as you did and provide details that illustrate your point of view.

Remember, communication is crucial when considering remarriage. There are no right or wrong answers—just clearly communicated and jointly understood issues that can play a significant role in developing a deep and satisfying marriage.

Questionnaire: Quotidian

Issues to consider:

1. I prefer a neat house where both help to keep things straightened up.

1	2	3	4	5	6
Strongly Disagree	Disagree	Somewhat Disagree	Somewhat Agree	Agree	Strongly Agree

2. I like to do a lot of traveling including international travel.

1	2	3	4	5	6
Strongly Disagree	Disagree	Somewhat Disagree	Somewhat Agree	Agree	Strongly Agree

3. I like to stay up late most nights to watch TV or read.

1	2	3	4	5	6
Strongly Disagree	Disagree	Somewhat Disagree	Somewhat Agree	Agree	Strongly Agree

4. I enjoy cooking and working in the kitchen especially by myself.

1	2	3	4	5	6
Strongly Disagree	Disagree	Somewhat Disagree	Somewhat Agree	Agree	Strongly Agree

5. I believe both should share in household and yard chores.

1	2	3	4	5	6
Strongly Disagree	Disagree	Somewhat Disagree	Somewhat Agree	Agree	Strongly Agree

6. I enjoy listening to music and have particular genres I like and dislike.

1	2	3	4	5	6
Strongly Disagree	Disagree	Somewhat Disagree	Somewhat Agree	Agree	Strongly Agree

7. I like to eat at similar times and three regular meals a day.

1	2	3	4	5	6
Strongly Disagree	Disagree	Somewhat Disagree	Somewhat Agree	Agree	Strongly Agree

8. I enjoy watching football on Sundays and several times during the weekday evenings.

1	2	3	4	5	6
Strongly Disagree	Disagree	Somewhat Disagree	Somewhat Agree	Agree	Strongly Agree

9. I consider myself very sociable and would enjoy meeting new friends.

1	2	3	4	5	6
Strongly Disagree	Disagree	Somewhat Disagree	Somewhat Agree	Agree	Strongly Agree

10. I have a number of hobbies. These could include hiking, going to the gym, camping, fishing, walking, reading, or a number of others.

1	2	3	4	5	6
Strongly Disagree	Disagree	Somewhat Disagree	Somewhat Agree	Agree	Strongly Agree

11. I tend to enjoy conflicts and don't mind arguing.

1	2	3	4	5	6
Strongly Disagree	Disagree	Somewhat Disagree	Somewhat Agree	Agree	Strongly Agree

There are additional discussion ideas found in the appendix.

Day-to-day activities have a significant effect on relationships. Your tastes on a neat house, what your eating style might be, and where you'd like to live are important issues to consider. We talked about the importance of discussing who's doing what, such as daily chores, cooking, and cleaning up afterward. We discussed travel tastes and nighttime habits and hobbies. Another all-important topic is exchanging memories of previous marriages and previous relationships. Are you willing to listen? Determining where you will live is also important to discuss early in the relationship. Lastly, how important is it to you that you win an argument?

The final chapter was a joy for us to write. We truly can say we're standing on the shoulders of our previous spouses. We've found it to be true that marriage can be as close to God's plan of a perfect marriage as it can be.

In the appendix, we've provided the complete questionnaires together. You might want to take the complete questionnaire before reading the final chapter. A reminder: after you read and answer the final questionnaire, consider all of them together and answer them honestly. Answer them separately and then come together and compare answers. Allow plenty of time to discuss them. We wish you the best!

Chapter Twelve ✦

How to Have a Charmed Marriage

♪ "At Last" ♪
Mark Gorden, Harry Warren

W e both have come to the realization that our most important relationship comes with our Savior, Jesus Christ. This
is the most permanent as well as important relationship you will
ever have. Though we love our spouses here on earth, we know it
is temporary. One day, each of us will leave this earth. There are no
marriages in heaven. Marriage on earth is a gift from God for us
to enjoy here. Our vertical relationship with God by far outshines
and deserves the most attention, and it will be the most permanent
relationship in your life and beyond this life.

We often say, "We're standing on the shoulders of our previous
spouses," because our previous marriages have benefited our present marriage. Although not perfect, our marriage is as very close to
perfection as life can be on this planet.

From Jim

I called my brother, John, to tell him the good news that I'd just met the woman I was sure I'd marry. I told him she was beautiful, charming, and the perfect one for me. And then I told him she'd been widowed twice.

"Don't'cha know they come in three's?" John joked.

I told Shirley his reaction, and she quipped, "Nope, the third time's the charm!"

And it has been just that. We feel incredibly blessed that we had a second—or in our case, a third chance at love and marriage. We believe our marriage is good because we learned from our previous marriages.

From Shirley

We still fondly remember our early days of marriage. To be honest, after six years, we feel like we're still on our honeymoon. The delight of waking up to a husband, lover, and partner is nearly indescribable.

It's true: some days I had enjoyed solitude. In my younger life, I longed for it. But in the past eight years with a two-year respite in between, I've found solitude highly overrated. I like being married.

Would you like a snippet of our life together?

Jim gets up first. He turns on lamps, lights candles, and starts a fire to take the early morning chill out of the room. He makes coffee, the pot chiming when ready. "How's the coffee?" he asks. Making my cup perfect is his goal.

Ahhh. The dark, French-roasted coffee with bubbles forming on the sides of the cup—always delightful.

We enjoy the fire. We talk quietly. Soon we open our Bibles and begin our daily reading. Jim says a quick prayer. "Heavenly Father, show us what you want us to learn this day as we read your Word." We record insights and prayer requests. Each day we pray for a different segment of our family: our combined eight children, grandchildren, and siblings. Jim's side one day, mine the next; each day a different side of the family.

Sometimes we talk all morning, looking at the clock in surprise to discover it is nearly lunchtime and we are still in our pajamas. Together, in addition to such long talks, we've experienced adventure, companionship, shared tasks, and long walks.

As the years accumulate, there is surprise and joy as we compare likes and dislikes. How could he not appreciate jazz? How could I turn up my nose at country music?

Our wedding vows were declarations we promised to keep.

For better for worse,
For richer for poorer,
In sickness and in health,
To love, and to cherish,
Till death do us part.

We've now celebrated six years and though we're no longer on "honeymoon drugs," we are still madly in love, grateful for each other.

Should you decide to marry again, here are eight areas of positive actions you can take that will make your marriage the best it can be.

1. Pray together.

Did you know that if a married couple prays together daily, there is a ninety-nine percent chance for success in that marriage? Ninety-nine. That is a heady statistic given by author and pastor, Craig Groeschel.[10] At Jim's suggestion, we prayed together aloud on our first date and it set a precedent. But you can start any time if you haven't prayed together just yet.

---

[10] Craig & Amy Groeschel, *From This Day Forward* (Zondervan, 2014).

If at first you are not comfortable praying aloud in front of someone, we recommend you sit together, hold hands, bow your heads and close your eyes and pray silently for a minute or two. When you feel comfortable doing that, start saying one sentence out loud, if only nothing more than, "Thank you for this day, dear Lord." The more you do it, the easier it becomes.

Some people are afraid to pray together because they think they're not spiritual enough. Simple prayers are fine. Certainly with God. We know praying together creates intimacy—spiritual intimacy. It naturally overflows to other aspects of your married life. Emotionally and physically.

Most likely you will begin to pray about other things. It is a wonderful, mystical moment in joining together with the Creator of the world and asking for his blessing on your day. On your family. On your marriage. On your world.

2. Communicate.

From Shirley

As we said above, both of us have benefited from our previous marriages. It took years in my marriage to Bill for us to learn to communicate. We struggled for twenty years, went to counseling and, after months of counseling, attended a couples communication class recommended by the counselor. I honestly didn't think anything would help because counseling so far had not made a dent in our struggling marriage, but this class did the trick.

Weekly, we were given tools to communicate. We read books and discussed them. We learned to listen carefully during conflict without interrupting. When the other person finished talking, instead of being defensive, we listened and repeated back what we heard. If we didn't hear it correctly, it was said again. We learned to be more honest—even if it hurt—while communicating our feelings in a respectful way. The honesty was freeing.

Bill's anger could make it hard for him to communicate. He

learned to say, "I'm angry right now. Please let me sort this out. Then we can set a time to talk."

Early in my marriage, I had read a lot of books that told me I was the one who needed to change. They advised me to "give in," "let him have his way," or "submit." True: I needed to change. But changing how I interacted with Bill made the most powerful difference.

I read, "For the Spirit God gave us does not make us timid, but gives us power, love and self-discipline" (2 Timothy 1:7 NIV). I asked the Holy Spirit to give me the strength not to fear Bill's reactions.

One afternoon, Bill came in the door with a frown on his face. "Hi, honey," I said, trying to sound cheerful. I attempted to greet him with a hug and kiss, but he stomped past and pushed me away.

"Just leave me alone," he growled.

Instead of responding as usual and thinking I'd done something to offend him, I decided to confront his anger. *What's the worst thing that can happen?* I took a deep breath and said in a calm voice, not sarcastic or angry, "Look, I'm not sure what's going on here, but I'm not going to take on your anger. You might have good reason to feel this way, but I know it isn't me." I left the room and started dinner.

A while later he stepped into the kitchen. "I'm not upset with you. It's something that happened at work. I'm really ticked—I'm going for a hike." He closed the door behind him, no longer as angry as he had been minutes earlier. My challenge to him had helped both of us. Though I had wanted to "fix" his feelings, I learned to give him space to work them out himself.

That communication class was the last marriage counseling class or session we ever attended. I can honestly say our marriage improved by eighty percent after taking the class and the last twenty years of our marriage were full of joy and greater commitment to each other.

〜

It is important to communicate regularly. Don't let things build up if something is bothering you.

Below are our rules in communicating:

- Keep voices level.
- If your partner is confronting you about something, repeat what they said. Keep the statement and repeat cycle going until both parties understand.
- Don't wait until you become really upset about something—or apologize right away if you know you spoke with sarcasm or angry voice.
- Keep the communication open by not getting defensive.
- Avoid the words "always" and "never."

3. Keep short accounts.

If you've done something to hurt/offend your partner, be honest and apologize—don't wait until you think it's the right time. If you're bothered or offended by something your partner says or does, don't be afraid to broach the subject.

Forgive. No one is perfect.

Appreciate often. "Thank you for the nice meal," or "You look really nice today," or "Thank you for emptying the dishwasher," or "Thank you for emptying the garbage." It's such an easy thing to do and means a lot.

4. Learn your partner's love language.

This is an excellent tool in learning how to really love your mate. After reading Gary Chapman's book *The Five Love Languag-*

es,[11] we learned what each of our languages were and then expressed our love in ways that spoke the way they heard expressions of love.

I learned my love language is "Acts of Service." I heard "I love you" when Jim helped me with tasks. It could be many things such as emptying the dishwasher, taking out the garbage, filling the gas tank of the car. Jim helps me vacuum the house weekly. He's a great sous chef, too! I love it that he clears up my messes as I prepare our dinner!

Jim learned his language is "Words of Affirmation," meaning love notes, me telling him what I enjoy about him. Spoken words are good, but I know notes written on a piece of paper speak to him the most. I observe him using one of my notes as a bookmark and he carefully saves every one of them.

You can take the love language test for free online. We think the principles make a lot of sense.[12]

5. Play together.

Sometimes playing together is enjoying a hobby, but it can also be landscaping a dream backyard, or remodeling your home. Planning and doing things together gives such a sense of accomplishment. Sometimes, remodeling can create more stress, but in Jim's previous marriage, it was just the ticket for saving their marriage.

Playing together might also be attending your favorite sporting event. Most areas have at least one professional or semi-professional team nearby, but there are always high school games to attend.

Perhaps it's doing something you may not enjoy as much as your partner. Shirley loves hiking and Jim goes along with her though it isn't his favorite activity. Together, you could join a community choir. Take a language class together. Take a dance class together. Go to the gym together.

---

[11] Gary Chapman, *The Five Love Languages* (Chicago, IL: Northfield Publishing, 2014).
[12] http://bit.ly/36CjZv7.

From Shirley

In my first marriage, my husband and I didn't play together much. It had the air of a business-type relationship: raising a family, paying bills, and living separate lives at the same address. After going through the communication class, we realized we didn't play together.

For years, Bill had done his thing and I had done mine. Now we purposed to have "planned pleasant activities," setting a date at least once a week to walk, go out for dinner, or get a cup of coffee together. We did those planned pleasant activities as well as learned a new hobby: mountaineering.

We took a mountaineering class, enjoying each step of the journey as we trained, shopped for gear, and made our graduation climb up Mt. Hood. It was something I'd never dreamed of doing and I liked it! I pushed back my fear of heights and edges to ascend the steep-edged trail. After that, we backpacked, rock climbed, and continued mountaineering. Our kids joined us for some adventures but many we did alone. This activity gradually transformed our relationship.

From Jim

Kathy and I were in an uncomfortable place in our marriage. We never did anything fun together, but focused on her career, my business, and raising our blended family. We argued and bickered. We were roommates on a treadmill, just pushing through each day.

As I shared in chapter 7, we found a place in the Columbia River Gorge that helped us focus on something together by purchasing a farm house that needed some loving care. Remodeling and developing neglected acres saved our marriage and established friendships that I still maintain in that small community. It helped our spiritual lives too; in the church where I served as an elder, we worked together in children's ministries.

6. Grow Spiritually Together.

It's important in a relationship to attend church together. You may both be attending the same church, or depending on where you live, you may find a different one. In our case, Jim joined Shirley's church when he relocated to her city. The important thing is to find a church you both feel comfortable in. Church attendance is extremely important in your spiritual growth as an individual as well as a couple. Join a small group. Volunteer where you're needed. In your new marriage, you may get a whole new set of friends to socialize with.

> And let us not hold aloof from our church meetings, as some do. Let us do all we can to help one another's faith, and this the more earnestly as we see the final day drawing ever nearer(Hebrews 10:25 Phillips).

Together, Jim and I share a passion and believe God has called us to minister to others who are grieving the death of a loved one. As we said in the introduction, twice a year we lead a thirteen-week grief support group at our church. We grow spiritually as we help individuals work through their grief and experience healing from their loss.

Read a book together that will build your spiritual muscles as well as build up your marriage. In addition to the *Love Language Devotional*[13] there are many devotional books available for couples to study.

7. Continue to date.

Often couples quit dating once they've said, "I do." But we recommend you take the time and effort to plan something that can qualify as a date every week. As an empty nester, you may not have

[13] Chapman, Gary, *The One Year Love Language Minute Devotional,* Tyndale House Publishers, 2009.

the need to get out of the house as during child-rearing years, but it's important to get out if you are able.

You dated before marriage. Why not afterward? It adds excitement to your relationship if you know something special is coming up. We like to take turns planning our dates. Here are a few suggestions:

- Explore local restaurants for "happy hour"; the rates are a lot less during this time. You can't lose!
- Take a hike. It can take only an hour or two to enjoy the great outdoors.
- Set a "no TV night" and read quietly together or play a game or put a puzzle together.
- Plan a romantic evening at home with candles, music, and a special meal—-and pretend you're staying at a glamorous hotel. Eat at your dining table or in front of the fire at a small table, start out with fresh sheets on the bed; light candles while you get ready for bed. Enjoy each other with soft music and the phone or television off.
- Go out for coffee and dessert.
- Take a stroll in the neighborhood and enjoy the sunset together.
- Attend a local concert. There are many available that feature local artists and aren't as expensive as big names.
- Watch a romantic movie.
- Take a mini vacation; go to Groupon or other websites that offer specials. Sometimes we'll go to the beach for a couple of nights during the week and enjoy a good price at a hotel with a view.
- Take the time for romance. Plan ahead and agree this will be "the night" to make love.

8. Cherish each moment.

In the wedding vows we shared with each other, we promised to "love and cherish." What does *cherish* mean?

Cherish: to hold or treat as dear; to care for tenderly; nurture.[14]

Hold dear every moment you have. Be thankful. Protect your relationship as though it were fine china. Next to your relationship to God, the relationship between you and your mate is the most important.

People often ask, "Aren't you afraid you'll have to go through grief again when one of you dies?"

We've learned from our own losses how quickly things can change. How like a flash that sometimes taken-for-granted clutch of the other's hand, the warm hug, snuggles in bed at night can vanish.

We tell them we are grateful for every moment we have with each other and consider it a gift for whatever time is allotted to us. Instead of focusing on the length of time together, enjoy every minute. We enjoy being a servant to the other. We treasure life itself. There is so much every day to be thankful for.

One day, one of us will leave earth for heaven. It will be difficult, but it's useless to worry about something that will eventually and inevitably happen. Both of us have learned God knows our days and knows the future. We've learned from experience that whatever happens, he will be with us through the valley. He promises us that. We will enjoy our precious time together, are grateful for every shared instant—and recommend you do that as well.

In our wedding program, we quoted C.S. Lewis, used with permission here:

> To love at all is to be vulnerable. Love anything and
> your heart will be wrung and possibly broken. If you
> want to make sure of keeping it intact you must give it

[14] *Random House Webster's College Dictionary* 2nd, ed. (1997), s.v. "Cherish."

to no one, not even an animal. Wrap it carefully round with hobbies and little luxuries; avoid all entanglements. Lock it up safe in the casket or coffin of your selfishness. But in that casket, safe, dark, motionless, airless, it will change. It will not be broken; it will become unbreakable, impenetrable, irredeemable. To love is to be vulnerable.[15]

We are grateful for our second chance at love and we wish the very best to you as you navigate the path to remarriage. We can say with full assurance we're overjoyed we met and married. ♪ At last . . . ♪

---

[15] C. S. Lewis, *The Four Loves* (Harcourt Brace, 1960), extract reprinted by permission.

Appendix I ∾

*F*or your convenience in this appendix, we included all the questions from each chapter. Here are some final thoughts regarding the questionnaires throughout the book. Keep in mind, there are no right or wrong answers. The statements were designed to assist you and your potential future mate to identify the common ground and areas of potential disagreements you may have which would prevent you having the relationship you desire.

Instructions to the Questionnaire

The Questionnaire can be taken by yourself or it is preferable if you answer the questionnaire separately first, and then share your answers and discuss any area of concern. Suggestions for discussing your answers are at the end of this instruction page. It is important to remember while answering the questionnaires to keep in mind what you are trying to accomplish. Discover possible insights into each other's personal values, goals, dreams, and daily habits that will lead to a satisfying long-term relationship.

Suggested Discussion Guide for Your Answers

Some suggested ways you and/or your potential mate might want to take a closer look when discussing your answers:

First, if you score a lot of 3's and 4's, that might indicate several vaguely veiled potential disagreements because there was neither strongly agreed nor disagreed statements of your preferences. Make sure you have fully discussed and analyzed any large gaps on a particular question such as one person rating a statement with a 1, 2, or 3, and the other person rating the same question 4, 5, or 6. Those could be potential "red flags" and down the road could be also be "deal breakers."

Second, if both of you are filling out the questionnaire, do this separately and then discuss your concerns with your potential partner. From your answers to the questionnaire, list what you feel could be the red flags (be honest!) to this potential relationship. Before you share these with your partner, you may want to list potential red flags with a good friend to make sure your answers are as honest as they can be. Be cautious, as you might be infatuated with romantic feelings and your answers may be biased, preventing you from honestly identifying potential red flags.

Third, you can also discuss areas of agreement that will assist in deepening your relationship.

When people are courting or starting a potential long-term relationship, they are acting out of their most gracious, flexible, and accommodating mindsets and mannerisms. Small issues now have the likelihood of becoming big issues after the honeymoon period.

You are now ready to start discussing the questionnaire after answering the questions below. Be honest. There are no right or wrong answers. Listen carefully, don't be defensive. Remember that your discussions are to assist you in deciding to continue the relationship and help you build a relationship you desire.

Chapter 4 Questionnaire: Moving Too Fast?

Refer to instructions in chapter 4, p. 66 questionnaire.

1. I think there might be red flags in our relationship.

1	2	3	4	5	6
Strongly Disagree	Disagree	Somewhat Disagree	Somewhat Agree	Agree	Strongly Agree

2. Am I ignoring red flags?

1	2	3	4	5	6
Strongly Disagree	Disagree	Somewhat Disagree	Somewhat Agree	Agree	Strongly Agree

3. Others believe I am ignoring red flags.

1	2	3	4	5	6
Strongly Disagree	Disagree	Somewhat Disagree	Somewhat Agree	Agree	Strongly Agree

4. I am working too hard to make the relationship work.

1	2	3	4	5	6
Strongly Disagree	Disagree	Somewhat Disagree	Somewhat Agree	Agree	Strongly Agree

5. My close friends or family believe I am moving too fast.

1	2	3	4	5	6
Strongly Disagree	Disagree	Somewhat Disagree	Somewhat Agree	Agree	Strongly Agree

6. My close friends and family are afraid this relationship will break my heart.

1	2	3	4	5	6
Strongly Disagree	Disagree	Somewhat Disagree	Somewhat Agree	Agree	Strongly Agree

Chapter 5 Questionnaire: Faith

Refer to instructions in chapter 5, p. 78 questionnaire.

1. We share the same background in our belief in God.

1	2	3	4	5	6
Strongly Disagree	Disagree	Somewhat Disagree	Somewhat Agree	Agree	Strongly Agree

2. I am comfortable in a traditional worship setting.

1	2	3	4	5	6
Strongly Disagree	Disagree	Somewhat Disagree	Somewhat Agree	Agree	Strongly Agree

3. I am comfortable in a charismatic/Pentecostal style of worship.

1	2	3	4	5	6
Strongly Disagree	Disagree	Somewhat Disagree	Somewhat Agree	Agree	Strongly Agree

4. We share the same Christian worship styles.

1	2	3	4	5	6
Strongly Disagree	Disagree	Somewhat Disagree	Somewhat Agree	Agree	Strongly Agree

5. I bring religious/biblical values into my daily decision making.

1	2	3	4	5	6
Strongly Disagree	Disagree	Somewhat Disagree	Somewhat Agree	Agree	Strongly Agree

6. Jesus Christ is an important aspect in my daily life.

1	2	3	4	5	6
Strongly Disagree	Disagree	Somewhat Disagree	Somewhat Agree	Agree	Strongly Agree

7. I wish to attend church on a regular basis.

1	2	3	4	5	6
Strongly Disagree	Disagree	Somewhat Disagree	Somewhat Agree	Agree	Strongly Agree

8. I am open to changing where I attend church to worship with my future spouse.

1	2	3	4	5	6
Strongly Disagree	Disagree	Somewhat Disagree	Somewhat Agree	Agree	Strongly Agree

Chapter 6 Questionnaire: What's Mine Is Yours?

Refer to instructions in chapter 6, p. 84 questionnaire.

1.   I believe in blending all our financial resources.

1	2	3	4	5	6
Strongly Disagree	Disagree	Somewhat Disagree	Somewhat Agree	Agree	Strongly Agree

2.   I have shared with my potential mate all my savings and debt I currently have.

1	2	3	4	5	6
Strongly Disagree	Disagree	Somewhat Disagree	Somewhat Agree	Agree	Strongly Agree

3.   I believe a prenuptial agreement might be helpful in describing our individual desires relating to how our financial resources will be shared.

1	2	3	4	5	6
Strongly Disagree	Disagree	Somewhat Disagree	Somewhat Agree	Agree	Strongly Agree

4.   I am willing to sign a prenuptial agreement.

1	2	3	4	5	6
Strongly Disagree	Disagree	Somewhat Disagree	Somewhat Agree	Agree	Strongly Agree

5. I have a "Will and Trust" and believe it would be helpful to draw one up for our relationship.

1	2	3	4	5	6
Strongly Disagree	Disagree	Somewhat Disagree	Somewhat Agree	Agree	Strongly Agree

6. I have a clear idea how we should share our daily and monthly expenses.

1	2	3	4	5	6
Strongly Disagree	Disagree	Somewhat Disagree	Somewhat Agree	Agree	Strongly Agree

7. I have financial plans for retirement.

1	2	3	4	5	6
Strongly Disagree	Disagree	Somewhat Disagree	Somewhat Agree	Agree	Strongly Agree

8. I have a clear understanding of what our housing arrangements would be (i.e. joint purchase of home, live in current home, etc.).

1	2	3	4	5	6
Strongly Disagree	Disagree	Somewhat Disagree	Somewhat Agree	Agree	Strongly Agree

Chapter 7 Questionnaire: Yours, Mine, Ours!
Blending Families

Refer to instructions in chapter 7, p. 102 questionnaire.

1. I like to spend a lot of time with my children and grand-kids.

1	2	3	4	5	6
Strongly Disagree	Disagree	Somewhat Disagree	Somewhat Agree	Agree	Strongly Agree

2. My children, grandkids, and relatives are a very important part of my life.

1	2	3	4	5	6
Strongly Disagree	Disagree	Somewhat Disagree	Somewhat Agree	Agree	Strongly Agree

3. I like to financially support my kids as the need arises.

1	2	3	4	5	6
Strongly Disagree	Disagree	Somewhat Disagree	Somewhat Agree	Agree	Strongly Agree

4. I like buying gifts for my kids and grandkids and my rel-atives.

1	2	3	4	5	6
Strongly Disagree	Disagree	Somewhat Disagree	Somewhat Agree	Agree	Strongly Agree

5. I like being involved with kids and grandkids and enjoy attending their various school and sports functions.

1	2	3	4	5	6
Strongly Disagree	Disagree	Somewhat Disagree	Somewhat Agree	Agree	Strongly Agree

6. I believe caring for my elderly parents is an important obligation presently or in the future.

1	2	3	4	5	6
Strongly Disagree	Disagree	Somewhat Disagree	Somewhat Agree	Agree	Strongly Agree

7. I am close to my siblings and it is important for me to maintain a close relationship with them.

1	2	3	4	5	6
Strongly Disagree	Disagree	Somewhat Disagree	Somewhat Agree	Agree	Strongly Agree

Chapter 8 Questionnaire: The Touchy Subject: Sex

Refer to instructions in chapter 8, p. 115 questionnaire.

1. I believe in abstaining from sex until after marriage.

1	2	3	4	5	6
Strongly Disagree	Disagree	Somewhat Disagree	Somewhat Agree	Agree	Strongly Agree

2. I have determined a specific point or boundary where I feel comfortable with physical intimacy (holding hands, kissing, petting and touch) before we are married.

1	2	3	4	5	6
Strongly Disagree	Disagree	Somewhat Disagree	Somewhat Agree	Agree	Strongly Agree

3. We have discussed what our physical/sexual boundaries are.

1	2	3	4	5	6
Strongly Disagree	Disagree	Somewhat Disagree	Somewhat Agree	Agree	Strongly Agree

4. It is both of our responsibility to maintain those boundaries.

1	2	3	4	5	6
Strongly Disagree	Disagree	Somewhat Disagree	Somewhat Agree	Agree	Strongly Agree

5. There is chemistry between us.

1	2	3	4	5	6
Strongly Disagree	Disagree	Somewhat Disagree	Somewhat Agree	Agree	Strongly Agree

6. I have clearly communicated my expectations regarding sex after marriage (frequency, who initiates, etc).

1	2	3	4	5	6
Strongly Disagree	Disagree	Somewhat Disagree	Somewhat Agree	Agree	Strongly Agree

7. We have discussed each of our desires regarding sex after marriage.

1	2	3	4	5	6
Strongly Disagree	Disagree	Somewhat Disagree	Somewhat Agree	Agree	Strongly Agree

Chapter 9 Questionnaire: In Sickness and in Health—Can You Say Those Vows?

Refer to instructions in chapter 9, page 133 questionnaire.

1. I have shared all major medical conditions or health issues I had in my lifetime.

1	2	3	4	5	6
Strongly Disagree	Disagree	Somewhat Disagree	Somewhat Agree	Agree	Strongly Agree

2. I have disclosed all the medications I am currently taking.

1	2	3	4	5	6
Strongly Disagree	Disagree	Somewhat Disagree	Somewhat Agree	Agree	Strongly Agree

3. I have shared all health-related issues I am currently experiencing.

1	2	3	4	5	6
Strongly Disagree	Disagree	Somewhat Disagree	Somewhat Agree	Agree	Strongly Agree

4. Staying physically fit is very important to me.

1	2	3	4	5	6
Strongly Disagree	Disagree	Somewhat Disagree	Somewhat Agree	Agree	Strongly Agree

5. I pay a lot of attention to my diet and nutrition.

1	2	3	4	5	6
Strongly Disagree	Disagree	Somewhat Disagree	Somewhat Agree	Agree	Strongly Agree

6. I would appreciate my spouse accompanying me to doctor visits.

1	2	3	4	5	6
Strongly Disagree	Disagree	Somewhat Disagree	Somewhat Agree	Agree	Strongly Agree

7. I have made specific plans on where I would like to be buried and the method: cremation or traditional burial.

1	2	3	4	5	6
Strongly Disagree	Disagree	Somewhat Disagree	Somewhat Agree	Agree	Strongly Agree

8. I have developed written "advance directives" so others know my wishes at my end of life. (Search the internet for many sample forms of advance directives for your state.)

1	2	3	4	5	6
Strongly Disagree	Disagree	Somewhat Disagree	Somewhat Agree	Agree	Strongly Agree

9. I believe there are many benefits to alternative medical approaches, i.e. vitamin supplements, chiropractic and naturopathic approaches to healing and healthcare.

1	2	3	4	5	6
Strongly Disagree	Disagree	Somewhat Disagree	Somewhat Agree	Agree	Strongly Agree

10. Some states have laws regarding "death with dignity," where physician-assisted dying are allowed. This is something I would consider.

1	2	3	4	5	6
Strongly Disagree	Disagree	Somewhat Disagree	Somewhat Agree	Agree	Strongly Agree

Chapter 10 Questionnaire: Politics: Can We Be Civil?

Refer to instructions in chapter 10, p. 142 questionnaire.

1. Politics are very important to me.

1	2	3	4	5	6
Strongly Disagree	Disagree	Somewhat Disagree	Somewhat Agree	Agree	Strongly Agree

2. Sharing my political party and agreeing on the platform is important to me.

1	2	3	4	5	6
Strongly Disagree	Disagree	Somewhat Disagree	Somewhat Agree	Agree	Strongly Agree

3. I enjoy watching cable news and/or listening to talk radio.

1	2	3	4	5	6
Strongly Disagree	Disagree	Somewhat Disagree	Somewhat Agree	Agree	Strongly Agree

4. I enjoy political discussions with my mate.

1	2	3	4	5	6
Strongly Disagree	Disagree	Somewhat Disagree	Somewhat Agree	Agree	Strongly Agree

5. I have core beliefs that are very important to me, such as: pro-life or pro-choice, monogamous marriage, and homo-sexuality.

1	2	3	4	5	6
Strongly Disagree	Disagree	Somewhat Disagree	Somewhat Agree	Agree	Strongly Agree

Chapter 11 Questionnaire: Quotidian

Refer to instructions in chapter 11, p. 148 questionnaire.

1. I prefer a neat house where both help to keep things straightened up.

1	2	3	4	5	6
Strongly Disagree	Disagree	Somewhat Disagree	Somewhat Agree	Agree	Strongly Agree

2.   I like to do a lot of traveling including international travel.

1	2	3	4	5	6
Strongly Disagree	Disagree	Somewhat Disagree	Somewhat Agree	Agree	Strongly Agree

3.   I like to stay up late most nights to watch TV or read.

1	2	3	4	5	6
Strongly Disagree	Disagree	Somewhat Disagree	Somewhat Agree	Agree	Strongly Agree

4.   I enjoy cooking and working in the kitchen, especially by myself.

1	2	3	4	5	6
Strongly Disagree	Disagree	Somewhat Disagree	Somewhat Agree	Agree	Strongly Agree

5.   I believe both should share in household and yard chores.

1	2	3	4	5	6
Strongly Disagree	Disagree	Somewhat Disagree	Somewhat Agree	Agree	Strongly Agree

6.   I enjoy listening to music and have particular genre I like and dislike.

1	2	3	4	5	6
Strongly Disagree	Disagree	Somewhat Disagree	Somewhat Agree	Agree	Strongly Agree

7. I like to eat at similar times and three regular meals a day.

1	2	3	4	5	6
Strongly Disagree	Disagree	Somewhat Disagree	Somewhat Agree	Agree	Strongly Agree

8. I enjoy watching football on Sundays and several times during the weekday evenings.

1	2	3	4	5	6
Strongly Disagree	Disagree	Somewhat Disagree	Somewhat Agree	Agree	Strongly Agree

9. I consider myself very sociable and would enjoy meeting new friends.

1	2	3	4	5	6
Strongly Disagree	Disagree	Somewhat Disagree	Somewhat Agree	Agree	Strongly Agree

10. I have a number of hobbies. These could include hiking, going to the gym, camping, fishing, walking, reading, or a number of others.

1	2	3	4	5	6
Strongly Disagree	Disagree	Somewhat Disagree	Somewhat Agree	Agree	Strongly Agree

11. I tend to enjoy conflicts and don't mind arguing.

1	2	3	4	5	6
Strongly Disagree	Disagree	Somewhat Disagree	Somewhat Agree	Agree	Strongly Agree

Remember, when people are courting they are acting out their most gracious, flexible, and accommodating mindsets and mannerisms. Small issues now have the likelihood of becoming big issues after the honeymoon period is over.

It is good to remember seeking relationship with someone is normal and good, but they cannot be the ultimate answer in our lives.

You are now ready to start discussing the questionnaire. Be honest. There are no right or wrong answers. Listen carefully, don't be defensive. Remember that your discussions are to assist you in determining if the relationship will continue and help you build a relationship you desire.

Our hope is that the questionnaires brought you many hours of enlightening conversation and learning about each other. Additionally, through this book, you and future spouse may have many years of fulfilling friendship and companionship. May God bless your budding relationship.

Appendix II

Jim and Shirley Mozena Timeline

James P. Mozena

Married Margi Siberz

March 22, 1969

Divorced, July, 1981

Married Kathy Epperson

October 22, 1983

Kathy died, July 25, 2011

Married Shirley, December 7, 2013

Shirley Quiring Mozena

Married Bill Rudberg

July 16, 1965

Bill died, February 3, 2006

Married Blair Graybill

August 16, 2008

Blair died, January 31, 2010

Married Jim, December 7, 2013

Other Books by Shirley

Second Chances at Life and Love, with Hope

When Shirley and Bill set out on a dream trip in the beautiful northwest wilderness to celebrate their 40th anniversary, what develops is a nightmare that has no end. Mysterious pangs turn into a vicious virus that makes its way into Bill's body. Shirley finds comfort through her Savior during the six months of Bill's illness—an illness which eventually takes his life.

After a time, Shirley's heart aches for companionship. Little does she know that living a few miles from her home, a widower mourns the loss of his wife of 32 years. They meet and fall hopelessly in love, and their love takes them on a two-year journey of joy and adventure until once again overwhelming heartbreak rocks Shirley's world. This is a story of faith and courtship to strengthen your own soul.

Praise for *Second Chances*:

This story is wonderfully written with honesty and the depth of understanding that only grief can bring. In spite of the sad story of loss, the message of the book is one of joy in the goodness of today and hope for a future with God.

—**Jan Pierce**, author

Be ready for an "all-nighter" once you open this book. Shirley shares her times of love, sorrow, joy, peace and renewal. Shirley's willingness to open her heart to help others is seen throughout the book.

—**Judi Mayfield**, author

I just finished reading Second Chances. *Thank you for sharing your story with authenticity and candor... your trust in our kind Father has been your bedrock...*

—**Diane Stevens**

***Second Chances* is available at Shirley's website (shirleymozena.com) or on amazon.com and barnesandnoble.com**

Beyond Second Chances

The true story of a woman, twice widowed, who finds fulfilling love again. After grappling with loneliness, Shirley enters a hasty courtship, and is crushed by a broken engagement just before the wedding. Once again, Shirley's dreams have been destroyed. In her grief, she fully surrenders to God, faces her challenges and learns to trust Him more deeply.

Praise for *Beyond Second Chances*:

I just finished your book and wish so much that I had read it BEFORE meeting you and Jim in Branson at Hope Restored. You are both living proof that our generous God does restore hope, because He loves us so personally.

—**Rona**, Colorado Springs, CO

***Beyond Second Chances* is available at Shirley's website (shirleymozena.com) or on amazon.com and barnesandnoble.com**

Order Information

To order additional copies of this book
or any of Shirley's books, please visit
www.shirleymozena.com.
Also available on Amazon.com
and BarnesandNoble.com.

www.ingramcontent.com/pod-product-compliance
Lightning Source LLC
Chambersburg PA
CBHW060519130626
46553CB00002B/570